MW01088230

BLESSED

....

STORIES ABOUT CAREGIVING

DAPHNE SIMPKINS

Quotidian Books
Montgomery, AL

Copyright © 2018 by Daphne Simpkins.

All rights reserved. No part of this publication may be reproduced, distributed or transmitted in any form or by any means, including photocopying, recording, or other electronic or mechanical methods, without the prior written permission of the publisher, except in the case of brief quotations embodied in critical reviews and certain other noncommercial uses permitted by copyright law. For permission requests, write to the publisher, addressed "Attention: Permissions Coordinator," at the address below.

Quotidian Books
Daphne Simpkins
Montgomery, AL

Blessed/ Daphne Simpkins. -- 1st ed.
ISBN 978-1-7320158-1-4

Contents

For Shelby Tennimon

and her parents

Lori and Dan Tennimon

Compassion—which means literally "to suffer with"—is the way to the truth that we are most ourselves, not when we differ from others, but when we are the same. Indeed the main spiritual question is not, "What difference do you make?" but "What do you have in common?" It is not "excelling" but "serving" that makes us most human. It is not proving ourselves to be better than others but confessing to be just like others that is the way to healing and reconciliation.

Henri Nouwen

GREETINGS

....

PROLOGUE

W hen I heard the story of an uncle who fought a shark to save his nephew, I was not surprised. Aunts and uncles and mamas and daddies and sons and daughters routinely put themselves between danger and someone loved. People understand and revere that kind of heroic love, but they often have different responses to caregiving love. Sacrificial caregiving love often has a taint of something else: unredemptive martyrdom; how'd you let yourself get trapped like that?; and the most withering and punishing of all is that mean word "codependent," which implies that you want to be needed so badly that you are giving more care than is required most likely to someone who isn't grateful.

None of those characterizations of caregiving is the whole and helpful truth about caregiving. Needing and giving care throughout our lives is an ongoing activity—not an aberration like fighting a shark or only a courteous reflex like saying "Bless you" after a sneeze.

Needing care is part of being human.

Giving care is love expressed.

Learning who you are as someone who needs and gives care is part of growing up and becoming who you were meant to be. We are all meant to be caregivers. I have been blessed to be a caregiver, and I have heard from others that they feel that they have learned more about love as a caregiver than other times in their lives. It can be a great blessing to give care and receive care.

What follows are stories about loving other people as yourself. They are not stories as dramatic as wrestling a shark to rescue a child. These stories are simply meant to show that caregiving isn't a stage of life meant to be outlived or only managed or called by another name to make it palatable although there are seasons of care where professional caregivers do what some of us cannot. There are also stories of innovative new ways that needs are being met in an aging population. You will find a taste of that in the story "Respite for Everyone."

Caregiving is a natural expression of love to others. When you do it, Jesus might talk about you behind your back. He talked about the Good Samaritan giving aid to a wounded traveler. Jesus called him a good neighbor. But when you look at that story carefully, you see that the Samaritan was simply a conscientious caregiver.

....

ONE

THE MIRACLE WALK

Dad was twenty-one years old when he became a landlord, a caregiver of transient renters by converting an old Southern mansion into an apartment building and himself into a landlord. The building he called by its street name--Alabama Street--stretched through the city block and was within walking distance of downtown Montgomery. Renting out apartments was a way of supporting himself and his mama, Florine Acosta, a woman that later we girls—his four daughters-- were taught to call Flo.

Alabama Street was seductive in a quintessential Southern way, with varying levels of many different shapes of rooms. There were four entrances, one on each side of the building. Two of these entrances led into the heart of the building—a foyer broad enough to be called a lobby.

Over time we kept company with ex-cons and righteous people. We lived among the sober and the drunk, and we had fellowship with the very poor and the well-to-do and the dark of skin and the whitest folks.

While we lived on Alabama Street, I was immensely happy. I liked the building my father had transformed into a home for so many people who worked hard like he did. I was proud of him and what I considered his invention of that huge home place for so many people who needed a home. Alabama Street was very big. I was as impressed with the size of it as I was the elements of architectural beauty that were aspects of the building's personality, its seductive allure. There were fascinating turns and banisters to slide down and French doors and transoms and stained-glass windows.

Best of all, there was a small room underneath the ground floor stairwell where a child-sized door led to what became my secret room. I worked there with my drawing tools in the small room where I also stored my broom and dust pan after I had swept the lobby, the hallways, and the front porch, jobs that had to be done every day.

I liked sweeping as I liked most kinds of labor. I particularly loved cleaning the stairs. I was only allowed to go upstairs to sweep. Entering the forbidden terrain of the next floor up lent the work a kind of mystery and excitement of being in the foreign world of strangers on the floor where I was not otherwise allowed. I took my time sweeping the stairs each day, savoring the ascent, pausing to listen-- to hear what was going on behind closed doors. I was a natural born eavesdropper, and I have never felt guilty about listening in on other people's lives. It was a trait I evidenced as a child, and which I have never given up.

Blessed

I knew the people who lived on Alabama Street by sight, although not all of them knew who I was or really saw me. As a child, I was invisible to many people and patted on the head or offered a stick of gum by others who sensed my presence as one does a light breeze blowing by and acknowledges it with some version of a wave.

Mr. Ashley was different. He knew me. He saw me. He lived in Apartment Number 3 on what was called the ground floor, but it was really one flight up from street level. The brown wooden stairs were wide and not steep, but they were still a challenge for Mr. Ashley. He walked stiffly in what appeared to be his entire wardrobe: tweedy gray suits with dress shirts. The collars of his shirts were frayed and a faded white. They matched in hue his coarse yellow-white hair.

In the beginning of our friendship, Mr. Ashley did not leave Alabama Street very often, and so he was starved for any news I could bring him. (We had only three primary television stations back then and nothing like the news channels that pervade our lives now.) Sometimes, when I finished sweeping the hallway, Mr. Ashley came to his doorway and handed me a Nehi grape drink, and I told him which of his neighbors had company the night before for dinner, and who was moving in and who was moving out.

Occasionally, Mr. Ashley asked me to do a small chore for him, like change a light bulb or reach something that had fallen and rolled underneath his couch. He could not stoop or stretch easily. He spent most of his time sitting in a chair by his window, for his apartment looked out over Scott Street, which ran behind and parallel to Alabama Street. From his kitchen window, Mr. Ashley could watch the fire station and the fire trucks come and go and his neighbors dart into the Scott Street grocery. He watched when the other tenants took their trash to the garbage cans that fitted snugly into the back left corner of the side yard. Sometimes, I took Mr. Ashley's trash out for him because it was a long walk from his apartment to the trash cans. Those times he usually offered me another cold drink—sometimes orange, sometimes strawberry. Although I knew my parents would not approve, I accepted.

I took slow sips of the fruity soda pop because Mr. Ashley gave them to me to buy himself some time with some company, and I, a working man's child, wanted him to get his money's worth. During one of our conversations, Mr. Ashley told me his deepest secret. "My dream these days is to take a good walk outside again."

I said immediately that I could go only as far as the street corner alone on Alabama Street without my mother's permission. He said, "My dear, I don't think I can walk that far," and I suggested, "We could try. We could go slow."

He smiled dreamily, fearfully, and his lips were dry and cracked. His teeth were his own.

We didn't take a walk that day.

And we didn't walk the next day.

Three days later I had to tell Mr. Ashley that I had raked the front yard, and he had to say that he would come and see what I had done. Then I had to say that some men were working on the street, but I couldn't tell what they were doing. He said maybe he could figure it out, and then I said, "Would you, 'cause I'm curious?" and he nodded cautiously, determinedly, as if he were ready to do me a favor for a change.

It took us a long time to reach the front door of the lobby of Alabama Street. In order to make it look like I walked slow all the time, I explained to Mr. Ashley how the light passing through the stained-glass window in the foyer could turn my skin different shades of colors, and he smiled, faintly. We stopped for him to catch his breath. While he was standing in the sunlight, he closed his eyes as if he were bathing in the colors. I closed my eyes too, and he said, "I can hear them," and I said, "I hear them too," because sometimes when I stood in the colored light coming through the stained-glass windows I could hear angels singing, but no one else had ever mentioned it to me before.

Mr. Ashley was the only person in my life who ever admitted he could hear angels singing. When the angels caught their breath, Mr. Ashley and I each caught ours, and we moved in sequence out the front door then and across the wide gray planks of the front porch and then down the flight of stairs that led to the street.

He did not lean on me. He gripped his cane, the fingers of his hand pale and not callused or rough like my father's, who did what he called "the real work of the world." Then, I whispered a prayer to God that Mr. Ashley and I could think of ourselves as walking on water, an idea that I got out of the Bible.

Almost immediately we were in a position to see what the men from the city were doing to the street. Several long breaths later, Mr. Ashley said, "They are lifting out the cobblestones to get to the water line, I think. Those old red cobblestones came to town as ballast on ships from the old country. You won't see them on just any street."

"You know a lot about streets?" I asked, as we turned and casually began the slow walk back to the house as if we hadn't done anything special. I would remember that moment for the rest of my life because it taught me what a miracle feels like—ordinary and extraordinary at the same time. It didn't have to be like the parting of the Red Sea; a miracle could feel like a slow walk with an old man in the sunshine.

"I used to know a little something about everything," he replied, sucking in his cheeks.

I think something inside of him must have started to hurt, because we didn't talk after that.

Once we were back at the base of the front steps, he closed his eyes. His head tilted back an inch, and I wasn't worried for even a second that he was about to faint. I know what it's like to want to feel the sun on your face and give in to that craving. Sometimes, I just stand still in the sunshine, and when I do, I think: 'I feel love.' And I don't know exactly what I mean by that, except sometimes words come out of me that I don't plan to say, but I trust what the Bible calls *utterances*.

After our first walk, Mr. Ashley was too tired to give me a cold drink from his ice box, and I was disappointed because I felt like I had earned a reward. It was only years later when I realized that desiring a reward for showing that you love others is not exactly a sin, but it is a fatal error in expectation. A lot of the time loving others doesn't give anything back, at least nothing tangible. I left Mr. Ashley alone, without saying his name again, and I closed the door to his apartment quietly behind me. I knew that he would take a nap, but it was going to be a dreaming sleep that would build his strength. As I walked away, I whispered to God, "Please don't let him be afraid he can't walk anymore."

My parents were unaware of the extent of my friendship with Mr. Ashley, although at night when they heard my prayers, I included his name at the end of the long list of relatives. No one asked me about him or offered a commentary. Life continued just like it always had after the miracle walk. I swept the floors. I drew pictures in my little studio underneath the stairs. And when my daddy went to collect the rent, he took me with him.

Mr. Ashley was one of the tenants who always paid his rent promptly. When we stopped at his door, Mr. Ashley opened it immediately, handing my father a small beige envelope with his name imprinted on the back flap and the exact rent amount in cash (fifty-five dollars) He never nodded to me in particular. Only as we walked away, I peeked back over my shoulder, and his eyes filled with gladness and joy. His attention followed all the steps that I took, and I knew that Mr. Ashley loved me.

Mr. Ashley was the first person I ever loved outside of my family. I loved him, and he loved me.

During the monthly rent collection, my father routinely inspected the hallway for debris and burned out light bulbs. I looked forward to going on the inspection tour with my father. I liked to be the one beside him, for he walked with confidence and energy. He often laughed at what I said, and I loved to be the one who made him laugh. He could grow serious though, and once he became very solemn right before he complimented my work. My father preached a prophecy over me that day. He said that I would always be a happy person. "You're smart enough to know that you are fighting a losing battle cleaning up after people, but you don't worry about it and you don't complain. Every day, you just go and sweep it all up again. I notice that about you. You will always be a happy girl," he said.

I didn't worry about the messes made every day. I moved the day's collection of dirt and trash from one step to the next, enjoying the solitude, the sense of accomplishment, and the colored lights passing through the stained-glass window that marked the division in floors midway between the two levels. Some days, I took my rest at that midpoint where the light spilled color at my feet, and I listened for the angels.

Whether I could hear them or not, I knew the angels were nearby just as the tenants lived behind their closed doors in the many rooms that were all around me.

Once, Mr. Ashley sat beside me on the brown stairs and asked me what I saw as I stared at the colored light, and I said, "I see music mostly. I mean, I hear it."

And he nodded seriously, and replied solemnly, "I see it too. Not always, and mostly with you, but I see the music too. And I hear it."

The language of beauty had a variety of names. Sometimes it flowed in me as colored light, and sometimes it looked like music or sounded like it, and sometimes--the best times--it was the springing up of words that came out of the thirst for Living Water and were uttered or hummed as prayers that drifted into heaven like smoke from a slow burning fire, passing through the angels themselves, flooding their dear heavenly faces in colored earth lights. It wasn't so much the substance of the prayers that mattered. It was the faith that caused the creation and which infused them with an energy to exist and soar upward to God, the Maker and Receiver of beauty's reports.

Oh, Beauty! It called my name early, and whatever form it assumed or demanded be born out of me, I gave myself over to it, marveling that even a small whisper of a prayer like the one I uttered for Mr. Ashley could bear what the Bible calls "fruit." For just like the story of Genesis where God spoke our world into being, we have the words to create. We need only speak and sometimes just whisper the words, dropping them like fruit seeds at the feet of God, and He can either make them grow or not.

It was my heart's hope and prayer that Mr. Ashley could take a long walk outside. Soon after our first trip together, he tried. He went slowly, and he didn't invite me for company or as a witness, but I watched him from the other side of the screen door inside the foyer where I was sweeping. I prayed a second time, "God, bring his old bones to life, like the ones from Ezekiel."

Before long, Mr. Ashley was walking a little further. He began by just walking to the next block where he sat on a bench at the bus stop. Buses would come by and stop, and he waved them on, because Mr. Ashley wasn't waiting for the bus in order to catch it. He liked to absorb the sight of so many people going places. It made him feel better. I admired that about Mr. Ashley. He didn't have to be going on a journey himself in order to enjoy the trips others were taking. He was a noble man, who got stronger from the sight of people living lives in motion.

Soon, he was walking all the way to town, where he began to have his lunch. Sometimes he went to Morrison's Cafeteria. Sometimes, he had a snack at The

Captain's Table in Belk Hudson; and sometimes, he would go to Chris' Hot Dogs.

Going out to lunch helped him. He walked to town but took a Red taxi home.

Sometimes I was on the front porch sweeping it off when Mr. Ashley arrived in his taxi, and then I would hurry down and sweep the walkway from the taxi to the porch, rushing ahead of him getting it ready for him. I would pretend to sweep faster and faster for him, leading the way up the porch, and he laughed and laughed the faster I swept.

Mr. Ashley was much happier after he began taking his walks to town and having lunch with other people. But he grew less interested in me, though he always spoke to me. I was never invisible to him. And once, when it suddenly occurred to him that he had not offered me a cold drink in a long time, Mr. Ashley held out a dime to me apologetically, in a hurry now to be going somewhere else. He said I could go across the street to the Scott Street grocery store and buy what I wanted, and I said, "No, thank you, sir," *because good girls don't take money from men.*

That day, he and I knew that whatever had been between us for a few months ended with the offer of his dime. I didn't resent the offer, and he wasn't embarrassed by my refusal, because in addition to the understanding that sunlight translated into colors by a special window looks like music and is set in the background of angels singing, he and I also trusted that there were seasons between people. Ours had mostly come to an end. A natural law got born in me: 'There are endings and beginnings that exist without requiring the judgment of being good or bad. The motion of living can be trusted.'

12

Which didn't mean that I didn't feel sad. Years later, I identified this sadness as grief; but when I was a child, I called it loneliness because I missed my friend, and maybe grief more rightly is that. There was this sadness, because his company and his need of me had been a special treat I looked forward to, but I had only to see Mr. Ashley walking off down the street with the sunshine of love on his back to remember that there was nothing to feel sad about really. Sometimes when a man gets strong enough to leave you it is exactly what should happen.

....

TWO

THE BEAUTY ROOM

After my baby brother died, Daddy got busy making his girls a beauty room in our new house on Edgemont Avenue. We needed to move from the apartment building on Alabama Street because we needed to live close enough to walk to school. Mother didn't drive. Bellingrath school was right across the street from our new house, and the room where we all got ready to go anywhere was on the opposite side of the house next to what had been for months the nursery. Our brother's nursery became the guest room again, and the laundry room to which it was connected expanded in its utility to become the beauty room. It's where we did our hair.

Daddy installed a pink sink with grey speckles like they have in real beauty parlors so that my sisters and I could wash each other's hair; and there was a stand-up rolling hair dryer which moved around the room to our various assigned chairs when it was our turn to sit under it. Our names were written in black magic marker underneath our chairs as if the colors alone would not be enough to declare its owner.

Mary Ellen's was Christmas red. Patty Kate's was royal blue. (Daddy called her Princess.) Mine was sunshine yellow. Mother used the small wooden chair with the white cushion that she pulled out from her sewing machine, and sometimes that was Julie's chair, too. Julie was the baby— a toddler, really.

We kept our hair rollers and jars of Dippety-do in our assigned drawers at the long pink communal dresser that stretched the width of the wall nearest the window. It had a big mirror, too, and there was plenty of space for cans of hairspray and rolling tissue papers that we used to ensure our hair dried evenly by being blotted and rolled securely around this paper. These little slips of paper poked out of our rollers, which then often fit snugly inside hairnets that held the rollers in place.

The only real problem we ever had in the beauty room was running out of hot water, and often the laundry waited until the rituals of baths and shampooing of five heads of hair had been completed. Then, the first load of towels would be washed. The never-ending cycle of laundry kept us company in the beauty room while we dried our hair or did our nails and while we watched our mother and daddy come back to life "After we lost the boy."

That phrase lingered in the air for a long time as my sisters and I tried to make it up to our parents that their hearts had been broken, and they tried to make it up to us that we had lost a brother. Our mother got busy doing odd jobs around the house. That's what she called them. And they were odd. She painted the originally yellow kitchen clock black and the grout around the cracked tile in the floor was painted a glossy black, too.

That's when Daddy took on the creation of the beauty room, his offering to us during this season of confusion and sadness. "I'm outnumbered," he'd laughingly explain when the room was showed off to a neighbor or one of mama's sisters, who laughed too because they were supposed to follow his lead.

Almost everybody saw through him, I think, but no one would say out loud that the beauty room was not only a consolation to us—beauty for ashes-- but an apology from dad lest we think at any level that he had really wanted that boy more than he would have wanted a girl. Or all his girls.

"I'm blessed," he would announce suddenly, jarringly. "We're blessed to have each other to love."

And heads would nod—rolled heads as we checked each other's reflections in the mirror, keeping the secret that mother was deeply silent and distant, and daddy wasn't himself--not yet.

Dad imitated himself the way he once had been, and we performed for him in the beauty room, a theater of sorts where we girls played out the parts assigned to us after we lost the boy. We washed our hair in his special sink, and we rolled our hair for him, enjoying the dresser and our drawers and our personalized chairs. We listened to the "Beatles" and to Mary Ellen, the oldest and our lead singer, offer commentary about aspects of romance celebrated in pop hits.

I always agreed with whatever Mary Ellen's viewpoint was. She was the family genius.

Patty, the family princess, would only watch us --her two older sisters-- and tilt her head sideways, studying us. "Maybe," she said, a thoughtful assessing answer that previewed psychology would become her field of inquiry. A lover of music, Julie, the baby of the family, danced in the way that a toddler moves to music.

Daddy would come by during our Saturday evenings in the beauty room and watch us wash and roll and dance with each other and start the laundry and stay together as the loads of laundry dried and then were folded onto the big table that flanked the other end of the room.

Most nights we weren't dancing for fun; we were dancing to convince him that we were happy too and that life was as pretty as a beauty room could make it. Daddy wanted to give us that assurance in the beauty room; we tried to give it right back.

Occasionally while his girls folded the clothes, separating them into the stacks to be distributed to separate bedrooms, tears sprang to his eyes, and he pretended they didn't. We pretended not to see.

Each week, after he left to take his bath and before he laid himself down to sleep earlier than the rest of us, one of us stealthily kidnapped his Sunday shoes from his bedroom closet. We took turns polishing his shoes for church. We washed his dress shirts and ironed them. We made sure that he had a clean white handkerchief in his pocket for church. We took care of him in our way. He took care of us and mama in his.

The girl whose turn it was to polish the shoes, returned them, moving stealthily like a burglar into his bedroom while he snored gently, a comforting sound that all was well. Then, pressing ever so slightly with her fingertips, she pushed the sliding wooden door of the closet back enough to place the shoes inside on the floor underneath his church-going suit that hung above. She'd leave the door just a little bit ajar so that the lingering aroma of that black shoe polish would not cling to his clothes.

Back in the beauty room, the drawers would be closed and all the papers put away. The chairs were pushed back against the wall and the folded towels and underwear picked up to be carried to separate bedrooms. Wordlessly Mary Ellen flipped off the radio while Patty Kate prepared the coffee pot for the next day. Julie hurried to her side of the bed in the pink bedroom she shared with Mary Ellen.

Patty and I shared the blue bedroom just across the hallway. Then in the night, with Daddy sleeping and mother solemnly working her crossword puzzle in the kitchen, Mary Ellen often sang a song for us.

She had a pure and beautiful voice that sounded to me like an angel singing in the next room. Her nightly lullaby was a constant reminder that beauty was doing its work, and over time, it did.

THREE

....

SAFE AT HOME

"I wish you wouldn't bathe the baby in the sink when it's threatening to rain," my father said.

"Where do you think I should bathe Katie?" my sister Patty asked. Katie was her first baby and my daddy's seventh grandchild since we had relocated from Montgomery to a small subdivision across the Alabama River in a house on 14 acres of land that my father bought and called the family woods.

"Why bathe her at all? How dirty could she be? It's not like she works for a living," Dad opined. He walked around the room restlessly when Katie got her bath.

"I'm going to bathe the baby," Patty stated flatly. "I promise I won't use up the hot water."

"It's not the hot water I'm worried about," he declared emphatically. "I'm afraid the baby will be struck by lightning while you're bathing her."

It was an honest concern. He had a lot of them. After raising four daughters and losing the boy, Dad knew a great deal more to be worried about in the care and tending of his grandchildren. Katie was his current pride and joy. Mine, too. I adored her.

"Do you honestly think Katie could get struck by lightning inside the house? In the sink? Before it even starts to rain?" Patty asked, tilting her head thoughtfully.

She was a fearless questioner of other people's motives and thinking—and a good listener.

Dad shrugged off the implicit criticism. "I did not create the laws of nature. I just know what they are, and water attracts lightning. That's my Precious Love you've got there in a sink full of water."

"I'll put my body between the window and Katie," the daughter this man used to call Princess promised. "If lightning strikes, it will hit me first."

That thought seemed to comfort my father temporarily; but after a moment, he argued, "But your hands will be wet, and you'll be holding my Precious Love."

"I promise that my body will absorb most of the electricity," Patty said, gamely turning on the kitchen faucet.

Seeing that the baby was going to be bathed over his protestations, Dad suggested, "Well, at least stand on the kitchen rug. It has a rubber bottom. Maybe that will help."

This conversation is typical of the child care discussions that take place around the newest grandchild.

Katie has brought out all of my father's nervousness about the pitfalls of baby-raising. These parental caveats range from how to bathe Katie to taking the child to the mall, where, in her stroller, this innocent victim, according to my father's view, is forced to breathe dust kicked up by oblivious shoppers.

"Why do you want to put a perfectly clean baby in the path of people and their miserable dirty feet?" Dad asked when Patty and Katie headed off to the mall last Saturday.

"We have to go somewhere," my sister said.

"Why?"

"Because the baby can't just stay home all the time."

"Why?"

"Because Katie finds other people interesting."

"Why?"

"I don't know why she likes other people. Katie is a social child. She likes to mingle."

"I think you're speaking for yourself and projecting onto the baby," my father theorized, stroking his chin thoughtfully.

Dad has picked up the word *projecting* from one of the talk shows. Dad's only previous experience with projecting has been the old-fashioned kind, when he showed those home movies of my three sisters and me at Eastertime standing in front of blooming azalea bushes and waving good-bye, though we were never really going anywhere.

My sister stifles a comeback, for she has seriously studied psychology, and she knows what's happening here. Our Pa is an anxious grandfather, obsessively cautious about the child he has dubbed Precious Love. (I had my own nickname for her. I call her Beloved.)

After the bath, Patty pushed the baby off in the stroller for a turn in the park. Our Pa stood at the window and watched his Princess and his Precious Love leave the safety of his fortress. His was a somber farewell speech: "I can't believe a child of mine would be fool enough to take my baby to the park. Think of the stray dogs that could be prowling, the squirrels that could be rabid, strangers with germs on their hands touching the swings' chains that the baby will hold, and then she'll put her hands in her mouth. Not to mention all that dirt. God, please help her."

Daddy prays out loud to God, who He knows always hears him. He thinks we don't.

"Katie will be fine," I promised him.

He looked at me with a fresh suspicion. "Sometimes, I don't know what to make of your sister."

I did. And being her sister, I attempted to redirect some of our father's anxiety from her to me. I confessed softly, "I take Katie to the grocery store sometimes."

Before he could launch into his warnings about the dangers lurking at Foodworld, lightning flashed across the sky and jagged threateningly toward the Village Green park. Thunder boomed. The neighborhood dogs began to howl. In my mind, I saw them gather-- those wild, howling potentially rabid beasts, head off in a stormy herd to the park, where they would attack and devour the innocent children playing there. Or, maybe this time my Beloved, Daddy's Precious Love would be struck by lightning.

I had meant to comfort my father--perhaps in time, to reason with him. Instead, I took my place beside him at the front door, and together we watched for the children to come home.

FOUR

....

SHOPPING WITH J. LO

Katie's small handprints mar the glass surface of the grocery's deli case. The deli manager frowns at the fingertips which trill across the glass, first here, then there. Katie has busy hands, like most ten-year olds.

"Katie," I say. "The lady just cleaned the glass. Don't touch it again."

Katie pirouettes over to me. "Can I have a piece of that ham to eat right now?" she asks expectantly. Her smile is sunny. Her greenish eyes peer up bright and with a hint of laughter in them. Her thick golden-brown hair is plaited on either side, and she is wearing a green bandanna that she found in the back seat of the car on the drive over here. She immediately tied the rag on her head to make a fashion statement.

"You can have some ham once we're in the car, although I could make you a whole sandwich at home," I prompt, because my instinct to keep her well fed is greater

25

than my desire to protect her from germs, to which, like the clean glass, she is oblivious.

"Why not right now?" she asks, sunnily.

"Not right now," I say, shaking my head, as we take our pound of deli ham and head toward the dairy case for milk.

My 10-year old niece doesn't walk to the next destination. Katie skips, while her hands move through the air as she practices over and over a movement that I can't place as part of a dance routine. A volleyball move? Basketball?

It is probably some dance move that Jennifer Lopez made popular with girls my niece's age. I like Jennifer Lopez, too, but I don't like her as much as my niece does who, upon being asked to write a story for English class, instantly contrived a scenario where she and J. Lo went shopping in the mall together. Katie read the story to me over fresh warm doughnuts Saturday morning, her small brown plastic eye glasses falling forward on her nose while she spoke aloud the envisioned fantasy of a great day of shopping with J. Lo.

"Good," I said, nodding.

My praise sent her downward over the paper to write nine more words. She counted them for me, her fingers moving across the page, feeling the words.

"Good job," I repeat, ruffling her hair with my hand. She is accustomed to my hands trailing her features, tousling her sun-kissed hair when it isn't plaited, and patting it when it is.

I like every style and move of hers.

Curious, she leans in, seeking answers behind the glass deli case.

Hungry, she asks to eat right there in the store.

Happy, she twirls, oblivious to the idea that older and less happy people find this kind of movement irritating.

"We need milk," I say, hoping to distract her long enough to get her home and feed her a proper lunch.

Katie skips up to the dairy case and finds a gallon, peering deep inside the case to check the date. Using both arms she carries the milk to our buggy, her body taking note of the feel of it against her chest. She grins in delight and says, with relishing wonder, "It's cold."

"Thank you," I say, as she lowers the jug of milk clumsily into the buggy, for there is only one kind of movement for taking out groceries and putting them in: clumsy. Grocery shopping is not a ballet.

I lean on the buggy, glad for its support, though I chide myself often that I am shifting into the posture of leaning on whatever is nearby. My niece does not know this type of self-consciousness yet. Her hands and feet work better than when she just began to walk and touch and bumble along on legs learning to stand. Most things Katie reached for went right to her mouth.

The germs! The germs! It has been my warning-- my lament-- for years, but so far my fear of germs has not taken root in this young girl who pulls the buggy to the check-out.

We stand in the check-out line. Her fingers trace the names of gum in the rack. She points to a Snickers bar, her favorite, and I nod, discreetly. She encroaches on the personal space of the shopper in front of us to grab it. Holding it, she closes her eyes and moans, "Love Snickers." She will place it on the conveyor belt, and once it is scanned, retrieve it immediately. She can't eat it until after lunch, but she will hold onto it until then. It is hers.

While waiting, Katie adjusts her bandanna and examines the phone cards that are hanging around us. Nearby shoppers wait for me to tell her to be still-- to learn the posture of stillness and self-containment that leads to leaning on buggies.

I suddenly see people like me as the enemy of the young and the energetic. Rather than rebuke her, I censor myself. I pull a piece of ham from the cellophane bag and hand it to her wordlessly. Delighted, Katie stuffs it in her mouth.

I ignore the unspoken criticism of others nearby, and work on standing upright. I can do it. The leaning is a habit I've drifted into, and I shouldn't have.

The poses of maturity often lead to this kind of inhibited posture. In the spirit of caregiving, we tell others to be afraid of germs, to stay still, to stay hungry until you can do something more polite about it until we grow too still and stay hungry so long we lose our appetites. Even being in a grocery store doesn't tempt us out of leaning on the maxims of constraining ourselves and others. I see the truth. We don't just nag others; we nag ourselves and call it the wisdom of delayed gratification. The adventure of being alive should not be buried under the rules of "wait, don't touch, don't taste, don't dance right now."

'Giving up dancing isn't wise, and growing older shouldn't be this still,' I decide in that moment.

J. Lo knows it, and so does my niece. Today, although I am my father's daughter, I decided I agreed with them.

FIVE

······································

I DREAMED OF HEAVEN

I am on hug restriction, monitoring my behavior as Katie and I have a day together in the mall, where we stop for lunch at a cafeteria, and the server behind the buffet line asks, "Does she want the child's plate?"

I nod almost imperceptibly, because although my niece doesn't think of herself as a child, I do.

Intent on making sure she gets blue Jell-O, my niece hurriedly orders fried chicken, ignoring the fact that they place a thigh on her plate and she will eat only legs. I say nothing. because she might think this is one of those instances when I am smothering her, embarrassing her. I wait it out.

We move carefully down the line, holding up as much traffic in the cafeteria as I do in the car. (I am the person other drivers yell at for being slow.)

Katie and I move carefully to the check-out, where the cashier rings for a waiter to help us get to a table. I can carry my tray, but Katie can't manage hers.

I do not hurry to go back after her, stealing looks over my shoulder to see if she can handle talking with the waiter. When she joins me at the table, she suggests matter-of-factly, "If I placed my drink on your tray, I could carry my own tray. It's the drink that I can't balance."

I nod thoughtfully, tipping the waiter a dollar. "That's a good idea. We'll do that next time."

We are having a good day, but I am already looking ahead to another day with Katie, another lunch, another time to look into her old soul eyes and connect with the girl who is the last part of my parents that I still have to enjoy--get to know.

I see her that way sometimes. Other times, she is a little kid, a young lady, my sister's daughter, and prissy the way her mother was at her age. I smile thinking of my prissy sister who gave us all this child to love. And just as I am in the midst of old maiden aunt reveries, I spy a man who looks just like my Uncle Sammy, who has been in heaven a long time now.

"Do you see that man?" I say, pointing over her shoulder. "He looks like your Uncle Sammy. He was a handsome man with a great smile. Did you ever meet him?" It is strange to have become the family historian. I often ruminate about people who aren't here anymore. I am happy to tell the stories of people who are a part of the family tree; but they are strangers in stories I tell that must feel like fiction to her.

"Maybe I met him," Katie says politely. "I don't eat chicken thighs. I eat only chicken legs," she says, looking puzzled. She eyes me curiously, as if I am a stranger. 'How did you slip up?'

I smile. I see that I am not supposed to hug her, but I am supposed to monitor her chicken dinner. I am learning the ever-evolving rules.

She is growing up, and I am learning to adjust. I send it back, not caring if it will cost more. Wouldn't I give her the moon if I could, and certainly a chicken leg?

I do not say this out loud any more than I permit myself to hug her up tightly at the very thought that she never met Uncle Sammy, a rather splendid fellow who loved us and was very good at Trivial Pursuit. He and I were always paired on family game nights, and made a lethal combination. That's not very important information, but it seems sacred somehow in this moment, this meal at a cafeteria where he would have eaten.

"Your grandmother really loved Sammy," I said, moving past the memory. "She loved all her brothers, but she had a special place in her heart for Sammy."

"I miss grandmother," Katie confessed as the chicken leg arrived. She dove upon it with the appetite that I enjoy seeing. I am hoping she will want another chicken leg so I can buy it for her.

"I had a dream about Uncle Sammy," I said while waiting. "It was right after he died. He was in a small cottage that was covered in ice that seemed lit up from within, kind of like holy ice, pure. I like to think the dream was a picture of heaven, and I could only see through the picture window, because I am still only here. He was so happy."

For a second I remembered what the dream felt like, to stand outside and look in and be glad that he who had suffered was smiling now. I did not talk about cancer or death, however.

"I dreamed of heaven once," Katie said, picking up a square of blue Jell-O. She eats this as prissily as her mother once upon a time ate dill pickles. Katie eats Jell-O squares with her fingers, her pinkie raised, the image incongruously ladylike and kidlike, and, well, adorable. I cast myself ahead to the future where I will be telling someone about Katie and the adorable way she ate the blue Jell-O squares.

"And what was heaven like in your dream?" I asked, scooping a forkful of black-eyed peas.

"All the houses were made of sunflowers and it snowed, but the snow was like glitter--not cold. Pretty. Falling all over me," she said simply.

"And did you see anyone you loved there?" I asked.

"Oh, yes," she admitted. "I saw every dog I've ever loved. I saw Rufus, Luke, and Gatsby. They were all there."

"You saw dogs in heaven?"

"All the dogs I've ever loved," she said, nodding seriously. She stopped to take a long sip of cola.

I drank water and sighed. "I don't suppose you saw any people in heaven?" I prompted.

"Oh, yes," as if people in heaven were an afterthought.

"The whole family is there," she said. "You are there," she said, using the present tense in a way that makes an English teacher uncomfortable but an aunt very happy.

I sat for that moment in a cafeteria and looked ahead to bright days of other banquets in other rooms covered in holy ice and what looks to a child like chill-less glitter and decked in sun-flowers, and I saw heaven through a child's eyes in that moment: we were there and we were going there, and it was a place where all the dogs and people I've ever loved are and ever will be.

"And when I woke up," Katie said, old soul eyes gleaming, small girl fingers touching blue Jell-O testing the texture, "I laughed."

....

SIX

FIGURING TIME

W hen the rain clouds form, I wonder where Katie is and if she's okay. She probably is. I am more afraid of her being afraid of storms than she is, really.

But when the winds pick up and the day turns suddenly dark, I flinch, holding back the impulse to go up and down the streets looking for her. She's not a runaway. She's in summer camp at the Y.

That's where she is all right. Where the pool is. And they swim in the mornings and again in the afternoons, I think. She'll be brown as a nut, and her hair will be as blond as it can get this side of heaven. That Katie! In my mind she still runs on the legs of a toddler; but in truth, she is almost as tall as I am. Her legs may be even longer than mine.

Tall for her age, her height declares that she has lived longer than she really has. Ten years old is not that old. Compare it to dog years or cat years or even rat years (she likes her rat science class)....she's still ten years old, human time.

But human time is not so easy to figure any more. The pace of technology pushes us to move faster than our legs can carry us--not faster than our thoughts can take us, but sometimes emotions don't adjust to an idea as fast as a brain can. There's a strange balance to seek. There is a heart adjustment to the progress of time lived out in children, who upon learning of our fears for them, actually laugh at us.

My sister's children do that. She told me so. Julie said that since her children have scattered to different time zones, she is always trying to place them in the schedule of their days while she is living out hers. She lives with them this way only under different roofs. "I'm up at 7; they're up at my 6. We eat at different times, later now for us on Eastern Standard Time."

But there is more to this sense of being late than living in a time zone that means all her favorite TV shows are on an hour later than Julie wants to watch them. Julie yawns through new nighttime episodes of *Law & Order* now, calculating when her distant babies will go to beddie-bye: that married daughter, her son in med school, and her youngest son Ben heads to college in the fall, but not another literal time zone, just the time zone of a young man who will be keeping on-my-own college hours rather than under-mother's-roof hours.

Julie knows what I mean. She figures time like I do. One eye on the clock, her mind trails the streets and other rooms where her grown children live--those places where we can't keep an eye on them, so we keep an eye on the clock, figuring time.

"You're always doing that," her daughter Jan laughed. "Figuring time like that."

Her son Ben agreed. "Everything gets compared to something else."

They think their mother is just a clock watcher. It's more than that. She sees them the way I see Katie every day while she's at camp or in her rat science class—watching the clock, imagining what she's doing, praying she's safe, and counting the minutes until I see the child's face again.

Mothers and aunts and fathers, too, figure time by a different instrument--the human heart. It's not as fast as technology, but it is a truer way of figuring time than any other timepiece.

SEVEN

....

EMERGENCY ONE ANGRY
WOMAN

She was a large angry woman with thick black hair who assumed that everyone in the emergency waiting room wanted to hear her opinions. Waiting on a friend who had cut her finger with the hedge clippers, I listened, watching as she sewed. Her red press-on fingernails flashed as she jabbed her needle ferociously in and out of her needlepoint.

"They aren't going to get in a hurry back there," she opined, referring to the medical staff in the back room where wounds were stitched and other maladies diagnosed. "But when it comes time to get their money, they'll be in a hurry then."

No one in the waiting room concurred. We all had medical emergencies in common--not points-of-view. A failure in any of the other people to respond did not deter the woman from continuing her diatribe.

"I'm forty-eight years old, and I've raised fourteen young uns. You see that boy over there," she said, motioning to a young man in a wheel chair. He was listening but pretending he wasn't. "Me and him collide. He's twenty-six and don't hold down a job yet. He goes fishing all the time."

She pierced me with black eyes, demanding I acknowledge the boy. I nodded to him, and he slouched down further in the chair. He had not acquired the defensive posture of self-consciousness that mentally competent people have.

"Fishing's not a bad way to spend your time if you can't work," I replied neutrally. "What kind of fish do you catch?" I asked him.

"Catfish," his mother answered for him. She sewed determinedly. Some point of satisfaction had been achieved by my interest in the fish, as if she were relieved of the idea that I might condemn her son for not working. For being a mama's boy. For being slow. For being sick today. "We caught ninety pounds the other day in one of those stocked catfish ponds. They charged us a dollar a pound."

"How can you afford it?" I asked impetuously. It sounded like an expensive hobby to me. Besides, wouldn't even the most fanatical of catfish eaters tire of the dish with ninety pounds to eat?

She ignored my question. "We put all the fish in the freezer with the turkeys and the venison. We spend about three months a year hunting ten thousand acres owned by a paper mill. Park our trailer there during hunting season."

Understanding dawned. This angry woman did not rely on grocery stores to feed her family.

"Do you hunt for your food?" I asked.

"Sure. Got me a gun this long." She motioned with her hands to indicate a yard's length. "Thought I was going to have to use it the other night. There was a big ruckus going on out in the woods back of the paper mill. Sparks flying higher than the pine trees. Thought it was a forest fire at first. Went to check it out. Turned out to be some big old teenage boys drinking and swapping drugs. They spoke nasty words out there in the dark. Anyone could hear them. I called the law on them. I'm a decent woman; and come midnight, I intend to get my sleep."

A nurse appeared to wheel the fisherboy into the back room. "I'll be right here," his mother promised.

He smiled loopily.

"Hurt my ankle," he explained softly, his brown eyes connecting with mine.

"I'm sorry," I said.

He smiled again, as if pain didn't matter. The doors closed behind him.

His mother continued. "I've raised fourteen children, and I don't let any young uns direct my steps, exceptin' my grandson. He got on the phone the other day and told me fat people die young. I let him put me on a diet. He asked me to exercise after every meal to help my metabolism work. Now, I get on the bike and pedal five, six miles at a time."

"You love your grandson very much."

Her eyes flooded. Tears began to stream, a release from the anger that was boiling within her. "He was born addicted to cocaine. I raised him the first three years of his life. His mama dumped him on my doorstep the day he was born. She come back two years ago and filed a motion to get him back. We went to court over it. Put her right up there on the stand. My lawyer caught her in a lie. The judge caught her in a lie. She's a known liar. Still, the court took that boy away from me and gave an innocent young un to a lying drug addict."

For the first time, the angry woman with so many opinions seemed confused about what was happening. The facts of life as she understood them were not being validated by her everyday experience. Her reason, her sense of ethics, her parental ambitions, were not prevailing to preserve the lives of people in her care. Only anger could do the job of expressing the rage of love this mother felt toward her young uns and a society with whom she was presently colliding.

"My grandson called me yesterday. Told me he's coming to live with me. Like he can just say that and make it come true." The needle began to move slowly. She pierced the cloth, gently now, her movements growing rhythmic, no longer colliding with the cloth.

"He says he's going to call me mama, and I told him, you can't do that cause Tammy's your mama, and he says he's gonna call her Mama-Tammy and me Mama." Her voice filled with wonder, with love.

"How old is the boy?" I asked.

"Six." Her eyes wandered to the closed doors where her other boy was having his ankle checked. Her bearing collapsed, as she considered the futures of her children. When she spoke, all trace of anger was gone. "He's got a long road ahead of him. I don't know how he's gonna make it."

I didn't ask her which boy she meant. This woman of many words did not speak again until I rose to leave. Then, she looked at me and said, "He'll be here in June. I'm exercising after every meal."

EIGHT

······························

FEVER PITCH

"He was sick all last week, and you know what that's like. He said he didn't have an appetite, which is just his way of saying that he won't eat anything normal. You know what that means?"

I grunted ambiguously into the telephone. It was a sufficient response to keep my friend talking about her ailing husband.

"Well, three meals a day, every day he was sick, I had to think of something special to fix for him to eat. And, of course, he couldn't come to the table to eat it. Wherever he was sitting, I had to take his food to him, and stand next to him while he ate the first bite because it might be too hot for him, and he didn't have the breath, he said, "to blow on my food." So I blew on it for him, and told him, "Don't burn your tongue, now darlin'.'

"Do you know how hard that is--to blow on someone else's food without spitting? I won't be winning any assertiveness training awards. But a woman can't argue with a man when he's sick because he's likely to curl up in a ball and die on her, and then she's stuck with the memory that she killed him."

Before I could verify that my friend really thought that her husband might kick the bucket if she told him no about anything, she offered another revelation.

"I can't tell you how many times I've imagined myself standing next to my husband's grave as we lowered his casket into the ground, and I'm thinking, 'This is my fault. If I could just have told him he was right one more time while he was sick, he might still be alive today.' Anyway, when he's ailing, I cook myself crazy trying to please him. Of course, it's a whole different ball game when I get sick," she declared. "He'll contradict me night and day because he thinks he knows what's good for me. I learned early on that when I'm sick, I might as well resign myself to dying or living on Saltine crackers because if I'm depending on my husband for food, I might as well join the birds outside and start hunting for worms.

"The last time I had a cold all I asked of my Sweet Thang was that he go to the store and buy me a can of chicken noodle soup. I begged him to buy me a simple can of noodley soup, because that's all I thought I could swallow.

"Do you know what he came back with? He brought back a can of that chunky beef stew with lardlike potatoes. He told me that the beef would be better for me than the chicken. When I told him that I did not think I could swallow hunks of grease, he actually told me I was being a difficult patient.

"To make up with him I had to tell him he was right one more time by eating every drop of that soup that he kept explaining he had made a special trip to the grocery store to buy. And you bet your life I couldn't stay sick for long. When he said he was going to go and buy me a case of that beef stew to last the week, I got myself out of the bed and told him I was all right, which I guess, means that in his own way, he did help me get well.

"He called me a few minutes ago. This was his first whole day back to work after being sick, and he said he was coming home for lunch and what was I making? I couldn't believe my ears. I don't cook a hot lunch except when he's here, and you'd think after all these years he would know that. I didn't tell him that though, because the news might have put him into a relapse, and I don't think I could live through that. I tried to break it to him easy. I said, `Don't you and the boys eat barbecue at the Smokehouse on Mondays?'

"He said in that low pitiful voice men get sometimes, `I want to come home.' You know how a man can say those words?"

"No, I don't," I replied truthfully. "I'm not married, remember?"

This was my first full sentence--okay, it was two sentences.

"I am," she replied thoughtfully. "And I love Sweet Thang to death and I'm glad he's well again; but when he gets here, I may have to shoot him."

NINE

....

MY CRANKY VALENTINE

The gentleman across from me in the out-patient hospital waiting room began rummaging in his pants for a pocket knife. His wife started to laugh when he pulled it out and unfolded the miniature screwdriver. "Now, don't you try to fix that coffeepot for those two sweet pink ladies. You'll just break it worse than it was before."

I looked behind me to see the woman speaking. His wife was a lovely woman with enormous laughing blue eyes and the kind of skin women over 50 don't usually have: firm, smooth, and a healthy pink.

The sick coffeepot in question was beside me on a table. It was in the care of two skittery hospital volunteers, who had somehow poured brewed coffee into the water well and messed up its insides. It wasn't an earth-shattering dilemma, but it was mercifully distracting in this hospital waiting room.

Before turning to go into the room where people in medical garb would check her blood pressure and poke her with needles, his wife waved an indulgent hand at me and cautioned teasingly, "Honey, don't you let that old man of mine break the coffeepot any worse than it already is."

I didn't say a word. I know better than to let myself get drawn into an old lovers' quarrel, even a good-natured one. My parents, married for forty-plus years, talk like these two old lovers do. They don't bicker exactly; but they don't bill and coo like the love birds they claimed they once were.

"What do you do?" I asked the would-be coffeepot repairman.

"I'm retired now," he said. "I sold tires." He told me how much he had loved his job; and when he spoke, he slipped into a gentlemanly shyness that harkened back to when he was a boy and awkward in the company of girls. I liked him.

"She," he said, motioning with his head toward the door his wife had exited, "can't stand having me around the house underfoot. Yesterday, I walked out to the back yard where she was to see if I could help her plant an azalea bush. My little lady looked up at me and said, `What do you think you're doing out here? Do you think I need you for this?'" He laughed with affection when he repeated the conversation.

Do you think I need you for this?

Would my blood run cold if someone I loved said those words to me? His did not. Her words to him sounded harsh to me, but his interpretation of them wasn't. To him, they were words of love. They reminded me of one of my parents' verbal exchanges.

Dad said to Mama: "You don't love me anymore."

Mama replied immediately: "I love you enough not to kill you even though you're bothering me while I'm working my crossword puzzle."

Daddy objected: "What do you have to complain about? Who else do you know who has a husband who still writes her love letters?"

Mama stated flatly: "You copied that last love poem out of a cartoon from the newspaper. Do you think I don't read the newspaper?"

Cackling with glee, Dad rubbed his hands together with satisfaction: "You fell for it just the same, Shorty."

A fledgling English teacher, I opined: "That's plagiarism, Dad. You'd get an `F' in English Composition for that."

They both looked at me as if I was crazy. Mine was not an appropriate comment to make to two people wrestling to continue creating who they are as a couple. Do psychologists have a name for people who can love each other all their lives without needing therapy?

I studied the retired salesman across from me. He was still fiddling with his pocket knife and eyeing the sick coffeepot. I could see an eagerness in him to fix it and prove his wife wrong, because then he would have something to tease her about later.

When his eyes met mine, I shook my head from side to side. He risked a sheepish grin and slipped the knife back into his pocket.

I saw his eyes flit anxiously to the clock. *Where was his wife? What was taking so long?* "Everyone told me I wouldn't be able to stand being retired and at home every day. But the second morning I didn't have to go to work, I adjusted," he said. "No phone ringing off the wall. No flat tires to fix. Just her to put up with." His eyes went to the clock again. *Where was she?*

The two hospital volunteers, who had broken the coffeepot, clucked sympathetically. It was their job to be sympathetic to someone in pain. But this man's statement wasn't an admission of the kind of pain they were thinking about. It wasn't codependency, not misplaced anger, not even the announcement of an armed truce between two people who have decided to stick it out till death they did part. It was a declaration of his undying love. It was the real thing, and time hadn't broken it.

Other than the coffeepot doing fruitless groaning, nothing in this room where people who love each other wait for each other, needed fixing.

TEN

....

HER MAGIC FOCUS

Upon inheriting my mother's desk since her death, I found an aged yellowed receipt for $263, the price of a case of mirrors called the Magic Focus. I remember the twenty-four mirrors she bought. I have the one she gave me. A girlish pale pink, it stands on a flexible base that adjusts to any position. It is wonderfully manipulative, designed to magnify a woman's eyebrows, her nose, any feature of her face that she needs to see better.

My mother discovered the happy benefits of the Magic Focus while on a trip and promptly ordered a whole case. The mirrors were not held back to be used as Christmas presents or dispersed deliberately as birthday gifts; they were given away immediately to her daughters and to any other woman she knew or heard about who would enjoy the gift of improved vision.

For a spell we were all under the spell of that Magic Focus, commending its benefits to one another. Days passed, and, of course, the mirrors were integrated into the routine of living called daily life.

It is the continuity of family life that I'm missing now. I find myself working at my mother's desk or studying my eyebrows for pruning, and I no longer have the security of being in a family that can expect the routine of living to continue. For until one loses a parent there is this comfortable misapprehension of a predictable future. Of some things remaining unchanged.

Nothing does.

One parent dies of a heart attack, and the other is diagnosed with Alzheimer's disease so that even the peculiarities of a father's nature are no longer viewed affectionately as his eccentricities but as symptoms of a deterioration that will not cease until his death. The popular statistics declaring the realities of heart disease and senile dementia are as real to me as the mirrors my mother bought to improve my eyesight.

I exist in this new motion of life called the presence of death with all of the artifacts that commemorate the lives of people who have been here and are now gone--or, like my father, are slowly taking their leave. I am caught off-guard by sudden discoveries of an old receipt and other unexpected discoveries like three bottles of Lemon Extract sitting on the Lazy Susan in my mama's spice cabinet. None of us can remember any recipe that called for that flavoring; yet, there must have been at least one pound cake or some other dish requiring a lot of Lemon Extract. But what was it? It is amazing how much I would love to know the answer.

The questions attending these discoveries bring a nostalgic gladness mixed with a sober grief, for we miss the presence of our mother's nature, her personality, the gifts of her spirit, which prompts occasionally this lament in me: "It's over now....the story that was us." What is left are artifacts and memories triggered by surprise discoveries like the old receipt for the case of mirrors bought years ago.

But the mirror, the receipt, the Lemon Extract are not unlike the sign posts of memory that cause me to stop on my way to get the newspaper and take in the knowledge of a clear blue sky. How often I saw my mother stop in her work outside, raise her arms to the sky, and greet the day as her own mother did.

Not three days after my mother's funeral, I sat outside on her front porch, my hands full of condolence cards, and I acknowledged with a surreal peace the beauty of creation and the cycle of life that we all participate in as best we can. My mother imparted this vision to me almost as casually, as generously, as she gave me a Magic Focus mirror long ago.

It is an unlikely focus--to know and in many ways have imbibed another's spirit so well as to override the loss inherent in death and the fear of greater losses to come. I dwell in this new land and declare that any single moment ripe with pain and dread can still be known as beautiful, nourishing, and sometimes because of its very brevity, enough of a magic focus to call the time of joy and pain here a very good life.

ELEVEN

....

LORI

Lori raised the newborn girl as high as her arms could reach, maintaining a balance that defied her confinement in a hospital bed.

"You are going to let me hold her?" I asked, incredulity rife in my voice.

"Of course," Lori said, handing over her day-old daughter Shelby with an alacrity that denied the truth of the hardship of the delivery. After nine stints in the hospital, Lori had her baby early.

"Thank you," I said, accepting the baby. There are times when I do not reach for children, nor do I hold them with the kind of unchecked gladness and affection with which I reached for this little girl. In part, my response to other women's children is shaped by pride. I do not want to look as if I envy them. Additionally, I know the discipline that single childless women teach themselves: I do not want to yearn for a baby.

Settling back in her hospital bed, Lori explained, "I had very little to do with the creation of that baby. She was a gift from God."

There was more to that admission than just the sacrifice of gratitude that women of faith believe in expressing when their hearts are full with joy. From handing me her child to admitting aloud that she didn't own the little girl called her daughter, my friend Lori was making herself practice living up to the vision she has of her future as a mother and her ability to manage the care of a child who will quickly outgrow her physical capabilities to tend her. Lori moves about in a wheelchair.

We had discussed this challenge of motherhood one night about four months into her pregnancy at a women's meeting. "I went to see a woman like me," Lori said, motioning dismissively to her partially compromised legs, hurt long ago when she was a younger woman. "She warned me that once a baby is big enough to scramble off your lap, you have to entrust them to someone else. It's the best thing for the baby, you see."

I see. Lori's view of motherhood is the same challenge my sisters and I face in caring for our father now whose illness—Alzheimer's disease-- has turned him into a six-foot toddler. I can envision a day that I cannot manage his care and must look for more hands than mine to do the job of protecting and caring for him. Unlike Lori's baby, however, who will grow up, my father will die ultimately of Alzheimer's disease. Sometimes when I allude to the time when I can't take care of my father, who has become like a child, my friends misunderstand and think that I will be glad to pass on the burden to someone else or give it up entirely. They are wrong. I am no happier to release him into another's care than Lori will like letting someone else do the work of taking care of her Shelby.

Some think his future death will release me from bondage to pursue once again my own ambitions. I have many essays I want to write, stories to tell, and I can type fast. "Trinkets from a fair," I think--nothing compared to loving well.

But presently, the pace of my heartbeat is better suited to keeping time with a seasoned friend in the hospital the day after her daughter is born. Rather than sadden me, it comforts me to hear hard truths. It comforts me to be one of the first women to whom Lori will hand her child and then lean back on her bed and catch her breath and wonder aloud how she will build back her strength. Swimming is the only aerobic activity she can do. There isn't a pool near us, and I think, 'I'll just have a pool put in at my house, and she can come over. She can work on her muscles in order to be able to hold her child a little longer, and I can try to swim off the grief that abides with me so that I can manage Dad's care for as long as humanly possible.'

I don't say it though; and for a few moments while I hold her baby Lori lapses into the ruminative silence that envelopes people who are serious about living authentic lives. We don't rush the silence. Instead, we simply and truly smile as a lady comes in to gather the trash from the room. I ask her, pointing at Shelby. "I know you work here and see a lot of newborns, but isn't this just about the prettiest baby you have ever seen?"

Entering into the spirit of rejoicing, she replied, grinning, "Oh, absolutely, and working here, I've seen a lot of babies. That one you're holding is particularly beautiful. A sight for these eyes."

Lori and I smile at the silliness of celebrating beauty. It is a conversational gambit, a moment of giving one's self over to being simply happy, to rejoicing over the goodness of being alive, to acknowledging the beauty of being together as the experience of being alive together unfolds. As always the experience of beauty's presence comforted me.

TWELVE

....

HER BODYGUARD

He stood behind his new bride at the dinner party, wearing the poker-faced expression of a caregiver who feigns invisibility until the patient in his care requires assistance. His too-thin wife sat in the only wing-back chair. Her legs splayed comfortably in an uninhibited posture that contrasted with the modest Southern-girl bonnet she wore to hide her bald head. His wife has breast cancer, and this man has become the vigilant caregiver--better, bodyguard--a job that seasoned lovers and good daughters usually adopt.

A former caregiver who spent three years locked inside a house with a father who suffered with and then died of Alzheimer's disease, I watched the bridegroom bodyguard, wondering in what ways his experience was different from mine.

My patient—my father-- lost his mind slowly. He forgot how to behave in public. He drooled and leaked. He got mad at hallucinations that stalked him. Sometimes strangers and his own kin feared him. In his dilapidated state, my father was not attractive to others. The isolation was acute for him and for me and my sisters.

During that time, I learned how to be alone in ways I did not know were possible. I learned how to wait, too. And, I learned how to do different jobs that are part of caregiving for an Alzheimer's patient: cut a man's hair, shave him, pare his nails. I even made friends with his delusions, which appeared as the sun set: "Sundowner's Syndrome," they called it.

I wondered about the new words in this man's life since the diagnosis of his wife's illness, and if he said the new words over to himself outside at night, practicing how to say them calmly when he had to—fearlessly when it mattered most.

A steady stream of well-wishers greeted the couple, attempting the awkward task of offering congratulations on the recent wedding while simultaneously offering words of sincere concern. I watched our mutual friends move through the room, making their way to pay their gentle respects to this sick bride, to embrace her, respectful of that side of her weakened now by muscle loss and radiation burns.

Her bodyguard remained poised behind her, silent, eyes disciplined and deliberately opaque so that no one could read his mind and see....what?

My eyes used to hide the secret life a caregiver lives. It is one of disciplined optimism. Of ready service. Of dread and hope living side by side. Of being terribly alone while always in the company of someone who was going to die no matter what I did as his caregiver.

'This caregiver has a more promising future,' I thought. The prognosis was good. Whenever possible one or the other of them said to anyone listening, "Get that mammogram. It's life or death. We caught it early." The treatments were working. And they had a network of friends who supported them. Those were the facts.

But was he still afraid? Did he have job pressures as he juggled caregiving with making a living that supported him and his wife? Did he feel all alone although, as a caregiver, he was rarely alone?

The buffet dinner was finally ready, and we all rose. His patient moved serenely through the crowd, a bride welcoming the guests at the reception. He followed her, nodding as others assured her that she looked great. She fixed her own plate, adding spoonsful of this and that, and I saw him watch and take deep breaths as she took more food. 'Good, good. Eat more,' he thought. 'Eat as much as you can.'

He forgot to make his own plate as he followed her. He smiled appropriately at friends who patted her or nodded some silent intention of good will toward him, but the smile never made it to his eyes. Compliments brought the bride closer to him, however. She leaned gratefully toward her husband, patted his chest, and called him her hero. The look in his eyes remained the same.

Suddenly, we were together in a corner, and I told her what everyone else had been saying-- that she looked lovely--and then I turned to him, the male counterpart to a focused, intense caregiver life I have survived and still think about as if it was a mysterious part of my past that doesn't need to be solved—just understood more and more as time passes in this new state the obituary named as being a survivor.

"How are *you*?" I asked him. It sounded like a casual question, the kind of question that everyone asks everyone. It is a question that always surprises caregivers because it is such a radical shift in focus.

This man, whose eyes had been opaque all evening, answered the question I have been wanting to ask about whether the caregiver experience is different for men than it is for women. It is the same. When addressed as a human being rather than as the silent stoic caregiving hero, this bodyguard answered the question with the same old word women caregivers use in order to save their strength for later. "Fine," he said, but his eyes filled with tears.

THIRTEEN

....

CONFESSIONS OF A
RECOVERING CAREGIVER

S ince my three-year stint as my father's caregiver, I wrestle with socially unacceptable urges to comfort, feed, and water just about anybody.

I do not have to know you personally to offer you a cough drop when you choke. I say "Bless you" before you finish sneezing, and my right hand will automatically fidget for an Aloe-enriched, bacteria-killing tissue.

After your third sneeze, I will tell you the names of cold products you need although these medicines are not only what I think promote healing. Sick people need to go to bed and rest and drink plenty of fluids and be waited on by people like me.

I am ready to do that. I am a recovering caregiver always on the lookout for someone who needs a caregiver—that is me. And I know that my attentions mostly wear on people's nerves.

My teenage niece Katie is tired of hearing me say, "Button up. Buckle up. Wash your hands." Sometimes I tire of hearing myself, but I cannot stop. It is cold outside, accidents do happen, and illness-bearing germs should be washed away.

This type of other-oriented watchful vigilance is not confined only to matters of wellness. Recently stuck in a bad traffic jam on the interstate, I opened my car trunk where I store some caregiving supplies and walked up and down the asphalt giving away free bottles of water to other stuck drivers. It was a very satisfying experience—so many thirsty people, and me with so much water to share.

That caregiver urge!—I overflow with it.

On an idling airport shuttle bus the other day, the driver asked the already seated passengers if we would be responsible to not let another person get on if he left the doors open so we could have fresh air while we watched.

Other passengers nodded politely. I got excited, for no one believes in the benefits of fresh air more than a recovering caregiver. I watched hard. Two people got on. I asked the lady beside me, "What are we supposed to do now?"

"It's not our job to guard that door," she said, shrugging.

My jaw dropped. I was envious of that shrug, for I have lost track of the boundaries of socially acceptable helpfulness, and I know it. I am labeled by others as codependent, hypervigilant, and addicted--one of those suckers born every minute.

But I wasn't born in a minute. My condition evolved over time while I handled medical emergencies for a dying man and forgot who I was, except as a caregiver. I have emerged from that experience in hyper-helpful mode. I watch. I warn. I offer. I am a recovering caregiver, and there's no twelve-step program to rehabilitate me.

But you could. And you could help others like me or who may become like me. First, you have to see caregivers. They live and move among you, but they are very adept at being invisible.

To find one, simply look beside a person suffering from age-related disorders or a debilitating disease. Beside a chronic patient is a barely alive, almost invisible caregiver. See that caregiver? Speak to him. To her. Speak these words slowly: "How are you?"

If she replies, "Fine," smile reassuringly. Send fresh fruit to her house anyway. Or send a fresh flower. Drop off fresh milk. Fresh bread. Her life is mostly stale, and she can't easily drive to a store for fresh stuff. You get the idea.

Does it seem like a small idea and, therefore, unnecessary? Think again.

Any gesture or gift of care for a current caregiver who has forgotten her own needs will become a potent memory that will surface later like medicine from a dissolving gel capsule that releases a healing dose of self-recognition and the restorative message: It's okay to accept help rather than only give it.

But don't over-react. If a recovering caregiver you know is already loose and roaming around compulsively offering Band-aids, water, cough drops, and tissues, don't resist her. Instead, simply accept everything a former caregiver offers, and say, "Thank you!" Caregivers haven't heard those words in ages.

Rather than feed an addiction for approval, which some experts warn is what makes caregivers who they are, that expression of simple courtesy will help a caregiver exhale and finally say to someone, "You're so very welcome."

The job is done then. See? She is finished. He can let go. Say good-bye.

I know. Every time I say those words, I say good-bye to my old caregiver self and breathe hello to the people who live in the world where I can imagine being on a shuttle bus sitting near a just-about-to-sneeze, almost-gonna-cough, possibly thirsty person, and--oh, bliss--simply shrug.

FOURTEEN

....

I SEE YOU

A lifetime snoop, I have always looked inside other shoppers' buggies to see if they are buying better groceries than I am. As a consequence, I was inadvertently trailing the woman who was now in front of me. We stopped in the dairy section where I heard her moan, "They don't have my yogurt!"

When her feverish eyes caught mine, I smiled sympathetically.

She raised her hands, exasperated. "They don't have my yogurt!"

"Is there some other brand you could eat?" I prompted.

"I can't get back here to the store. I've got a sitter taking care of my husband who is crazy! Crazy! You don't know." She shook her head as if clearing visions that she wanted to forget.

"You're probably right," I agreed soothingly.

She took a deep breath and tried to read the names of the other brands of yogurt.

"I like low-fat yogurt," she said. "With peaches. Not this custard stuff."

"Have you tried the custard stuff?" I asked gently. "Because it's pretty good."

"I just want my yogurt." She almost stamped her foot.

I didn't blame her. When a caregiver's life has gotten way out of her control, she wants something simple, like her peach yogurt, and it doesn't seem fair that she can't have it.

"I know," I said, reaching past her for the custard stuff.

"I don't usually look like this," she said waving a red chapped hand at her outfit.

It wasn't pretty. She wore an old jogging suit, and the top didn't match the bottoms. Her walking shoes were dirty, and the cuffs of her pants were covered in red dust.

"I've been for a walk, and I really needed that walk. I'm trying to live," she exclaimed.

I nodded, positioning my buggy to leave, but the nervous lady stopped me. "My husband has Alzheimer's disease, and I've hired a new woman to sit with him so I can take a walk and buy my peach low-fat yogurt, and I won't be able to get back to the grocery store until I don't know when."

I nodded silently.

"He's my second husband. We haven't been married very long, just two years. I've placed calls to his oldest son, but he doesn't return them. I need help!" She said the words as if she thought I'd argue otherwise.

"You do need help. You can't do it alone," I assured her. "No one can."

She focused on me, her face pale, the skin tight with tension, no laughter in her haunted eyes at all--not even the memory of it. I knew that look. I used to wear her expression and a version of the same outfit she had on. I wanted to buy her a bottle of Gold Bond lotion for her hands.

"My father had Alzheimer's," I said softly. "It's hard. Keep calling his son and hire all the help you can. You really can't do it alone. Consider Assisted Living. They can help you."

She inched closer, as if I had forgiven her of some trespass. "Could I ask you something horrible?"

"Yes," I said.

"It's an awful question," she warned me fiercely.

"Ask it," I said.

"My husband....my husband," she repeated the words emphatically, "propositioned the lady who was taking care of him before. I got an emergency call on my cell phone, and she was yelling hysterically. I hurried home and asked my husband what he had done. He drew back and said clear as a bell, `Obviously I was mistaken about her intentions. She was being awfully fresh with me though.' How could he do that? How could he talk like that—so normal and do something so shocking?!"

"Alzheimer's patients can do shocking things and sound normal too," I replied.

"And he has cursed people. He knows curse words I've never heard! Who did I marry?" She screeched.

Other shoppers heard her and scurried away.

"You married a man who was probably already sick and is getting sicker," I said gently, because I remember that it was hard to hear other people talk to me. I didn't think anyone understood anything at all about the way it is to live with an Alzheimer's patient. In order to survive, one must try to understand what it's like in the alternative reality of the patient: what dementiaville must be like. One must be able to navigate it while not taking up permanent citizenship there. Tough duty. "My daddy had Alzheimer's. I took care of him," I say.

"And your Daddy said awful, awful things?" she asked.

"Sometimes," I said. "It was a stage that passed. Another stage took its place that was shocking in a different way." At the time it all felt traumatic. Shocking and heartbreaking. Now, when I remember those days I see that they were really more messy than tragic. It was one more mess after another to clean up day after day.

"That's good to know," she affirmed. "It helps."

We pushed our buggies toward the check-out where the woman got right in front of me without apology and reached aggressively for a couple of packages of cigarettes. Yogurt and cigarettes. I could see how she needed them both.

She answered the cashier's routine questions quickly, her eyes darting toward the door. She was already headed home; she just wasn't in the car yet. I knew that focus: that sense of urgency that is suspended and then suddenly returns like a fever that spikes because you've left your patient at home and he might need you to protect him from others—to protect him from himself. Or herself.

When it was my turn to check out the cashier said, "That was nice of you to let her go first. A lot of people come in here, and they are in such a hurry."

"I see them," I said, as I watched the woman who was like the old me get in her car and peel wildly onto the street. The caregiver thought she was invisible—that people only saw her sick, shocking husband, but I saw the newlywed caregiver, and I could see the future and how she would be again.

I wanted to call after her, "You're not the only one it's happening to, and you really will be all right again."

FIFTEEN

....

THE ACTIVITY DIRECTOR

I was praying my way along on a drive to Birmingham to speak at an assisted living home when suddenly sublime communion happened. Just before the hail storm hit, I knew a moment of ecstasy.

Later I would try to understand if something in that routine prayer had been a catalyst for transcendence into sublime joy and communion with God. (It's not easy to describe ecstasy because to do so puts it necessarily in the past tense, and ecstasy is about being fully alive in the moment.)

So, there I am in the car, praying for the salvation of souls belonging to Craig, Cheryl, and a string of other acquaintances, when the ecstasy hits and gratitude flows out of me so fast I know that I am running out of words and begin to wonder, a question that shimmers just behind the coursing ecstasy: 'What happens after the words run out?'

In ecstasy, I go from rushing words to sublime desert silence and then back to the present moment when I realize that I need to pay attention to my driving directions to the assisted living home where I am scheduled as the three o'clock activity. This place has a formal, grandiose name that reminds me of the people of my church. There the newborns are christened with long names that belonged to important or wealthy ancestors. I marvel at such names, for my own was snagged fifty years ago off the air waves from a song on an old radio program "Hit Parade." My parents told of capturing my name as it went by in its vaporous way, and said joyfully in anticipation of the next new life coming, "Let's call the next girl that." So Adam, so Eve—naming the new animal, me.

I think of this moment warmly, going back to a time when my parents were alive, and I wonder if they could have been happy in an assisted living place, fancy name or not. They both died fairly young at home—mama from a heart attack three years before Alzheimer's would take Dad. I wonder if I will one day live in a place with a fancy name since I have no children, as if that is the determinant. I have many friends with children, and many adult successful children take no great protective or even an affectionate interest in their parents. We may all end up in the same kind of assisted living place with a fancy name or a cuddly name or a sentimental title—descriptive names chosen to evoke warm, safe, companionable, and sometimes grand feelings meant to be a consolation for growing old in America.

As the child of a real estate man who wrote the advertisements to sell his properties, I know about packaging a piece of real estate. Assisted living establishments that serve an aging population, like planned communities designed and built to support younger families, have an identity built out of words assigned by someone with a marketing vision. The builders of these places, however, are not the people who create the quality of life for the older residents. The person who shapes the quality of life for older folks who live in these cozy cottages or in green meadow-y establishments is often the Activity Director.

The Activity Directors are the administrators who call me on the fly and book me in a hurry. They are always, always very busy, often running late, have lost the information to introduce me when I arrive, don't have a microphone available or a glass of water for me (I carry my own bottled water), and they are very good at their jobs.

For it is not their preparation for a visiting speaker that tells the story of what they do. Their attention to the residents instead of everything else that could distract them reflects their devotion to the quality of life they are trying to build for the people under their roof, like a good mother does every day.

On a tight budget (liquid soap dispensers thinned, no paper towels in the bathrooms), and little supportive technology or people to help them set up and serve, the Activity Directors of assisted living homes plan meeting times and other social occasions that their residents can participate in and be enriched or stimulated by. Sometimes they sponsor a beauty pageant or host sing-alongs. They bake cinnamon rolls together with the residents, and sometimes they invite me to talk about popular culture topics.

This day I am a speaker for the twice monthly afternoon tea hosted in a setting called the Grand Ballroom. It is a weathered old lobby of a converted hotel. The refreshments are laid out with care. I espy a fruit topped cream-filled cake, hot coffee, fresh pineapple, and little crustless sandwiches, which this Activity Director makes sure she explains have turkey inside instead of beef because of Shirley's objection last time to beef.

As the Activity Director explains the menu change, I recall how my sister Julie modifies family dishes to accommodate a new daughter-in-law's taste or when a daughter gets pregnant and appetites shift. It matters little, really, that a dish's recipe changes; what matters is that someone in charge of the quality of life has cared enough to pay attention to what someone doesn't like. Or does. It isn't just atmosphere suggested by names and titles; it's personal preferences addressed. It's what we're all afraid will stop happening for us as we lose more and more control of our physical environments.

I give my recipe-rich speech about the many faces of Betty Crocker, a woman who never lived, and Aunt Jemima, a woman who never lived either. Both icons affected American culture and challenged homemakers but were alive only as the marketing brainchild of corporate businessmen. The speech goes its own way, adapting to the audience, and the residents come alive with memories of good times. They are mostly relishing telling someone about stack cakes and drying apples on sunbaked tin roofs and how good New North Cookies once were and how they were made with ingredients which were affectionately measured in pinches of this and lumps of that. The size of the hand didn't matter.

I set aside the assessment of myself and my still-evolving speech and go to make my good-byes, warmly receiving and returning the embrace of the Assistant Activity Director, Pearl, who is a Christian—something we know about each other instantly and almost immediately confirm. She tells me that she has just recovered from a lumbar problem.

"God helped me," she testifies.

I report that I am still getting well from shingles. "Christ has been so close," I say.

Pearl and I make the kind of homey conversation newly acquainted sisters in Christ share to affirm that we understand one another's recent trials, and I don't ask her if she has experienced any ecstasy lately. You can talk so easily about illness and suffering often associated with growing older, but not ecstasy, and only joy when it is polite joy—the kind that fits the occasion. I have known unspeakable joy in a hail storm today, and I don't tell anybody.

The Director closes the occasion by reminding everyone of the choir practice and the bingo game, where there will be prizes, and the trip to Walmart, which will not run so long that they can't make it back to choir practice.

"You have a good life worked out here," I tell Pearl, and just as I do, I hear my mother whisper from heaven: "You can live an awfully long time in this world."

I know what mama meant better now than I did when she first said it twenty years ago, ten years before she died while taking care of Dad, who had Alzheimer's. Taking care of Dad wore mother's heart out before the dementia stole my daddy. My sisters and I took care of him when he was growing old too fast, and I wrote about the experience in a memoir, *The Long Good Night,* which feels now like an old photograph, even an old recipe, from a long time ago now. These days I spend different kinds of afternoons with older people, and though my family experience was rich in dementia and simultaneously the paradoxical abiding always orderly peace of Christ, my broader encounters with other older people outside my own family have taught me that there are reasons to be hopeful in all the seasons of our lives.

As anyone does who has qualified for membership with AARP or senior discounts at the bank, I look ahead to the end of my days and wonder which assisted living rooms will be mine and will there be afternoon teas and company or dementia and pain and human isolation? Will the grand piano be played or silent? Will there be a draped plastic tube that drips fluids into my arm while I rest on a bed that is too cold and where the sheets are all washed in disinfectants? My fair skin is severely allergic to harsh soaps and chemicals, and I wonder if there is any way I can write all that down for the caregivers of me to come; and if I do, will they read it?

I have not done so yet, having witnessed that many times the ailments that plague us during our lives fade away in old age. My grandmother Ruby Pearl Morris had terrible arthritis that seemed to disappear when Alzheimer's claimed her, and my daddy had heart trouble that was swallowed up by Alzheimer's as well.

Growing older has its rewards and other events of hopefulness that no one reports much. I guess we think we are being insensitive or ill-mannered to inquire of the aged what the blessings are, but I visit many places where the inhabitants are older, and they are blessed and do bless.

I want to live out my days like that, but I don't have an elaborate plan that will make it happen. My recipe for growing older has a pinch of insurance and a lump of security and the repeated mantra often prayed in sunshine and in rain, "Jesus, I trust you with my life." My real plan is my only hope, which is in the One who has kept me so far:

the One who doesn't age but who will keep me company as I grow older. He knows our frames and our skin conditions and the old recipes and who our helpers will be who will choose the menus that our bodies now need. He has kept us company in the valleys and introduced us to that other state no one talks about much—ecstasy, unlikely ecstasy that came to me in a hail storm on my way to an assisted living place with the One who invented Activity Directors and called them to their work as he has called me to mine—and you to yours.

On the drive home from Birmingham, stuck in five o'clock traffic in a city a hundred miles from my own bed, unable to race the thunder and lightning storm that replaced the hail storm, I think about that as the winds increase and begin to buffet my petite red Honda Civic. I pray my way safely into the ongoing traffic, my car rocking, the wheels wanting to hydroplane and the moment of ecstasy experienced earlier in the day still shimmering incongruously inside of me, looking for words to shape it into a recipe that I can repeat, because who wouldn't want more ecstasy?

But I know better. I cannot cook up ecstasy for myself. That experience of the presence of God is a gift. Trying to learn a way to produce effects of grace on command is a human impulse that got Adam into trouble and creates the fear that many of us flirt with when thinking ahead to the days when we are older than we are in this moment and won't be in control of our menus and may be living in a place we didn't choose or name.

But we won't be growing older alone. We all grow older with the One who doesn't. Instantly, faith triggers gratitude and becomes a hymn of praise for the abundant life in Christ that Pearl and I acknowledged today. A grateful life is possible all the days of our Jesus-saved lives.

We receive and taste it though: this life of grace with streams of blessings hoped for, sought, and paradoxically found just as it is promised in the Word where he says, "We will make our home with you."

In all the homes of our lives.

On the road in a hail storm and later in the wind and rain.

In old hotel lobbies now optimistically renamed Grand Ballrooms.

In a room for one where there was once a happy couple, at midnight or midmorning, in our youth and when we are no longer young.

I am no longer young, and I knew ecstasy again today. I do not need more ecstasy to be content with the life given by my Creator (I can be abased. Ask anyone who has had shingles or lived with Alzheimer's in the house); but I report the abounding, and I suspect that sublime joy continues to happen to others all their lives too though people may not be able to speak about it easily.

We talk about the faithfulness of God so companionably during times of trial and tribulation, but there is more to life in Christ than pain and persevering. He makes each day's activity good in its way. The One who came to fix what Adam broke knows how to do it every day for each one of us all our lives long. He promised. He has all that He needs to do it.

And no matter what our age or where we live, Jesus does not stop.

SIXTEEN

....

THE WISDOM
OF ASSISTED LIVING

Recently a very articulate, very independent older friend of mine did some rehabilitation time in an assisted living home (probably the best one in town, and we know all of them), and though younger than she, I have always had a Nancy Drew kind of brain, and so I impertinently asked Marge, "What was it like?"

Back in her own home now, Marge can afford to assess how it was and could be again, for that is the question. She answered thoughtfully, sorting the words, "I was there two weeks and three days."

That specific answer revealed a lot. She repeated the number three more times when I asked about how the aides were and did she maintain her privacy.

"I kept my door open," she said, chin jutting up.

They can't take away your privacy if you willingly give it, I translated.

"How was the food?" I asked, for that is the single most important question that gets asked of assisted living managers.

"It was all right," she said. "I don't really want to spend the rest of my life thinking about salt, sugar, and whether I like the food. Sometimes you just have to eat what is put before you and give thanks."

"Do they say grace at the assisted living home?"

"Some do. Mostly privately, which I like. Heads go down and come back up pretty fast. If the head doesn't come back up fast enough, someone nudges the person cause he's napping. A lot of people nap in assisted living homes."

"You didn't."

"No. I was wide awake a lot of the time. I was surprised by how many people I knew who lived there permanently," she confessed. "I saw a man who was my first neighbor in town, and it was good to see him. So many of our church friends live there now."

True. Our church, which is big on church planting, has through this shift in the aged population of our membership sort of planted a satellite church of us over at this assisted living place. We don't send a van for them on Sunday mornings though.

"A lot of people enjoy the talking in the common room. There was a lot of talking…." My friend's voice trailed off.

"Too much talking for you?" I inquired for we both enjoy a solitary temperament, silence broken up by honest communication between people of shared good will.

"No," she said, her blue eyes brightening. "My family is a big group of talkers. We love words. There, they…" she faltered. "The talking among the residents was often gossipy, and even saying this makes me sound gossipy, too. But they were often so very judgmental of each other and the staff. When your days are numbered, why spend your life and time and words talking meanly about other people?" Marge shrugged and said, "But look at me. I'm doing that right now."

"It's okay to tell the truth," I said softly.

"They talked about each other. I don't need to hear that."

I wondered then if she minded my asking her so many questions. *Were questions like this offensive, and if so, should I stop?*

"Like I said, I was there two weeks and three days. Here's how I got through it. I said to myself, 'Get real.'"

"What does that mean?" I asked.

"It means, get real," Marge answered flatly.

I nodded as if I were capable of getting real in the way she intended.

"And I told myself, 'Life is not just about you here.'"

"That's a tough one," I affirmed. "Anywhere you live."

She nodded succinctly. "And then I told myself, 'You've had your turn. Accept what is.'"

Oh. I gulped as a woman at a nearby table in the restaurant asked the waiter to turn on the silent TV.

My friend stopped talking to me to say to her, "You can watch TV when you get home. This is a public place. Don't turn on that TV," she directed the waiter.

He read her gaze and backed away. I stifled a grin. Marge's turn wasn't quite over yet.

"I've seen a lot of older people become tyrants," she assessed thoughtfully. "I don't want to be a tyrant. But I really don't like to hear a TV playing in a public place. I like to be with live people more. I liked that about assisted living."

"So, ultimately, what did you take away from your two weeks and three days in an assisted living place?" I asked point blank.

She assessed me, answered slowly, not at the pace of advanced age but at the speed of considered thought—wisdom. "I learned I could make a good life there if I ever need to do it full time," she said.

And Marge sat back in her chair and smiled.

SEVENTEEN

GINNIE AND HER
BINGO GAMES

D on't start coming to visit a resident at a nursing home or assisted living place unless you are going to keep coming.

I read that advisory in a memoir written by a professional caregiver who was concerned about meeting the needs of people who have been installed there by relatives who could not do the work of providing good care.

I go to assisted living homes for a variety of reasons, but most often, for personal ones. I have independent minded friends who set their own boundaries of how much care they want by choosing assisted living and like where they live.

And I have a friend who is in assisted living and who needs as much help as she can attract from Outsiders, which is the name the residents at her assisted living home use about the people who come to visit. I've been checking on Ginnie a long time, and I'm still an Outsider.

When she's playing bingo, Ginnie tells me "I'll just be an hour—wait over there."

Sometimes I do wait. I'm very good at waiting. But yesterday I told my friend Ginnie that I didn't want to watch her play bingo again. I have watched an astonishing number of residents play a version of this prize-winning game that is not like the brand they play on cruise ships where people sip chocolate martinis and play $20 game cards for big awards. (I cruised. I played. I won. I have known the wonder of bingo.)

But it is a different game in assisted living and nursing homes where the callers are minimum wage aides who have stopped in the routine of laundry, cooking, and housekeeping to spin a small wire basket and call out the numbers very loudly without all of the funny in-between talk, jokes, and chit chat that are the hallmarks of a pro bingo emcee on board a cruise ship or even at the charity games where ginger ale with cherries in it is served.

They don't serve ginger ale with cherries in the assisted living home today. The caller isn't funny or cute—won't hug or flirt with you—and the markers that cover the numbers are sometimes dried beans or poker chips and, today, Fritos.

It is that type of bingo that my friend Ginnie plays in assisted living, and it is that kind of bingo she won't stop playing if I call and ask if it is convenient to drop by. It is the type that they play often and all week long in each of the cottages that make up the larger establishment where she lives, which is on my way home from work.

I was headed home from work mid-Friday afternoon when I called again, believing that I was an hour early for bingo, but they were having an earlier game in a different cottage. Ginnie was there, and she said, "You can come by. We'll be through by 3 PM."

At a quarter of two, after a long morning in meetings, I was ready to be home--not sit and watch a bingo game--so that's what I said, and Ginnie didn't mind. It didn't register with her that the length of a bingo game to her was an hour of precious solitude for me, an hour to rest before the work of the evening begins: the laundry, the cooking of the evening meal, the wash up, the evening bath, the preparation of my personal kitchen for the next day with a quick inventory about breakfast, lunch—and what would be for supper the next day?

My friend does not understand my sense of time. I am glad she likes bingo, but I wonder what it must feel like to no longer remember that the world at large does not treat its citizens as if it is populated by caregivers who live to give care. In the world of Outsiders, we fend for ourselves, hunt and gather, and try to take goodies and news from the outside world into the different world of assisted living, where Pepperidge Farm cookies, microwavable popcorn, a hot rotisserie chicken, a fresh Honey Crisp apple, and Welch's grape juice are desired and hard to come by.

Usually I take something like this to Ginnie in plastic bags that she can recycle as trash bags since the establishment no longer provides them (they are belt-tightening too).

She is always glad to receive, but never offers me a glass of water or asks questions about my life, work, troubles, or health. Instead, she spills the details of her life, mostly complaints about ill-treatment, which resemble in form and tone the whining of some of my long-time colleagues at work who think that the demands of teaching cost them more than they are willing to give and for which they are not adequately compensated or appreciated.

In that way, my friend in assisted living sounds like a couple of my co-workers.

Sometimes I would like to sound like that to my friend: unload some of the burdens of my day in the company of someone who will listen; but she has never asked me. I marvel that even the simple courtesy of inquiring is no longer a part of her social routine.

When someone comes to the door and taps, she names the chores she wants done, the menu she prefers and on the schedule she expects because she is paying for the service.

I admire that about her as often as I marvel at it, for while it appears to be a disagreeable side of what Outsiders call selfish, obstinate, hard-headed behavior, I think it is that very stubbornness that has helped Ginnie to survive alone in strange places for years now. She has few of the tools of self-preservation that help us Outsiders: money, mobility, the cache of independence and forward motion that we value as the energy of progress. Rather, she has her will, her demands, her resolute fortitude expressed with both small feet on petite legs balanced staunchly, like a captain of a ship in front of the wheel, except she is holding onto the two sides of a silver metal walker.

So yesterday I told Ginnie I'd call her again soon, and she hung up fast because bingo was happening—a routine game where the prize is a quarter. I marveled as I pressed the End button on my cell phone that her choice to keep playing rather than welcome a faithful visitor who had treats for her was poor economics. I am wrong, of course. I am thinking like an Outsider, for what I think I'm bringing is, in capitalist terms, more valuable than a quarter win at bingo, but what she's really choosing and winning in that moment is the right to say yes and no as often as she can in as many ways as she prefers.

I think about her as I head home, stopping for a fresh Honey Crisp apple for me and mushrooms for my evening salad in a light early winter rain that makes me want to be home sooner than I can get there. My routine chores await me. I get them done. Tired from a long day of hard work, I sleep on clean sheets that I changed myself and wake up to the solitude that I prefer above most things in life, and sit on my sofa drinking morning coffee, praying through my to-do list and wondering how my friend's day will be. I wonder how long Ginnie will continue to enjoy bingo there and the other ways that she has adapted to a kind of assisted living that an Outsider cannot ever truly imagine.

I will call her in a day or two and ask. If she isn't too busy, I will drop by. Once upon a time, I was afraid to start visiting friends in assisted living for fear that it would be so hard to do that I wouldn't last and then I would disappoint them—and myself. But I am not afraid of that any more than I am the well-intentioned advice and warnings that one reads about how to be a good visitor to people in assisted living homes written by people who believe themselves to be in the know of what Insiders prefer.

The boundaries of etiquette that connect the world of Insiders and Outsiders in assisted living establishments are far more flexible than most people believe—as flexible as the many ways that a game of bingo can be played.

....

EIGHTEEN

LIBBY

"They have pots of flowers at Walmart," my friend reminded me as we veered toward a nursing home where our friend Libby was recovering from a fall.

"It goes against my religion to go to Walmart," I replied stoutly. Some days I can stand Walmart; other days, I really can't.

"What religion is that?" my best friend of 30 years asked tartly. She is also my Sunday School teacher and has every right to quiz me about such matters.

"I believe in remembering widows and orphans," I replied rapidly, as traffic whizzed by. "And in keeping myself unspotted from the world," I muttered darkly as a patrol car cut us off while attempting to catch up with a lawbreaker to whom he wanted to give a ticket.

I waved my hands excitedly. "Go ahead and kill us in the name of traffic safety!" I screeched.

"Stop that. He'll turn around and give me a ticket."

"You haven't done anything wrong," I replied, lowering my hands. I believe her. A policeman who will cut you off in traffic will give you a ticket just to keep you in your place.

The world is full of relationships like that—a form of power brokering that keeps people in the lanes prescribed for them by people who are healthier and have more power or volition.

"I'm not going to tell you how to drive anymore today," I promise as she takes a surprising right turn and heads in a direction I had not anticipated.

She bursts out laughing. "I've been meaning to ask you….what is it about you and those widows and orphans?"

"What do you think we're doing right now?" I replied.

"We're going to see a friend who has experienced a fall."

Neither of us adds to that. We know what will most likely happen next. We have plenty of friends who have experienced a fall, and that's usually the beginning of what we describe next as "going down."

We say this during the prayer request times in Sunday School and now on Wednesday nights, too, which have added a prayer time for the sick.

We stop at a store other than Walmart and buy a pot of red and yellow zinnias and make our way to a popular nursing home and park underneath the best shade tree. Wordless now we tramp across the parking lot, speaking brightly to two ladies sitting outside in the breeze and who eye the flowers voraciously, like hungry people would devour with their eyes a plate of home fried chicken.

The clerk knows the room number of our friend without looking it up, and we are both reassured. It is a very good sign when the staff knows the names and room numbers of its residents.

My friend reaches Libby's door first and taps decorously. It is the same knock she uses on hospital doors and the prayer parlor at church before entering. It is her *Is it okay if I come in?* knock.

"Who is it?" Libby rasps.

Libby sees us before she can process our names, which we both call out. She pulls herself up in bed, fixing the expression of laxity on her face to one of welcome.

I watch her struggle. It is not a small thing to regain one's composure while in a recuperative hospital bed where all the accessories of our mature public selves have been stripped away, and we are left as we really are: physically weak for a spell. And in Libby's case, too thin.

There are the same big splotchy purple bruises on her legs and arms that seem to be on many older people. The cause is bumping her shins against the walker while taking some kind of blood thinner, I surmise. But I do not know. I have simply gotten used to seeing these types of bruises.

Her hairdo is worn-out, and she fluffs the back of it self-consciously, reaching down to tug at her pajama pants that are showing too much leg and those bruises.

"You are so sweet to come and see me," Libby says, and her voice is sand-papery from not talking much. "Sit down. Sit down."

For that moment, a visitor to a patient in assisted living doesn't really know how welcome she is. But at this moment, she takes a chair and settles in, doing first what is hardest to do: try not to look in a hurry to leave.

I want to leave, and I fight to look as if I don't.

I settled in with resolve, with the same gritty determination that this friend and other friends have tapped into when suddenly the women they have been portraying themselves to be can't be performed, and they must be revealed as this: a vulnerable waiting person who eats what is brought and who has a variety of explanations for why her children don't come to see her. The excuses roll off her tongue: "They are so busy. The real blessing is that they're so happy in their lives."

My friend and I make the clucking noises of affirmation that allow her to keep this guise in place while we quiz her about her health, her pains, and what her doctors say.

"I could get out of here if the pain would let up," she says, and her eyes cut to the window where the world is waiting for her, isn't it?

"Shall we pray for you?" I ask.

That is my job. I suggest the prayer, but my best friend Guin is the one who launches mightily into a stream of beseechments that call upon perfect mercy to descend and heal.

I hold Libby's hand while we all pray, and her hand is thin, but I can feel her pulse beating strongly. My shoulders ease. I control a slow exhale.

My friend finishes praying. I add a few extra requests from God, and we all say amen.

Guin and I struggle to our feet, trying not to groan as our respective weights shift upward to standing, and our friend lets go of herself some--leans back, her eyes brighter now, and she sighs, "I think I'll get better now. I believe I will."

She could.

I've seen people come out of nursing homes and go back to what they call independent living.

I know the labels. I know what they mean. Their boundaries. But I also know the nature of this confinement and how so much of getting better can depend on just how much the person in that hospital bed wants to recover—feels missed, desires to get back out there, not riding a cruise ship or jogging on Nikes (just do it) but feels desired and welcomed to reenter the gentle sway of life just outside these doors.

"Is that Katherine's room down the hall?"

"Yes. But Kat died. They haven't taken the name tag off yet."

We pause, offering a response of silence for this other friend who has passed on, waiting for the rhythm of respect to shift again to the place of encouragement and hope. My eyes drift, and I see blood stains on the sheets where my friend has been poked and bled and inconveniently soiled the sheets that have not been changed. I wonder when it happened and how long she will sleep on them.

She refuses to see the bloodstains, meeting my gaze that returns to her as I hand her my card with my phone number on it. "Call me if you need anything. I'll come back and take care of it," I promise.

It is a bold statement to make, but I make it routinely now. It's the way I say good-bye.

NINETEEN

....

RESPITE FOR EVERYONE

"He's addicted," she whispers in my ear, and when she says it her head ducks in a move I haven't figured out yet. Humility? Discretion? A quirky body language move of her own that means, *I'm thinking*?

"I don't have any friends anymore. I have her on speed dial," Daphne Johnston says next, pointing to an older lady across the meeting room who is engaged in helping one of the people who comes to the Respite center during the week in order to get some socializing and give the caregiver at home some time to him or herself.

"I live and breathe this ministry now," Daphne J. says, pointing toward a volleyball net that the volunteers are setting up for a game of balloon volleyball. It is the next scheduled activity of an action-packed day at Respite.

The guests of Respite and the volunteers who work here gather automatically, knowing what to do in their way. Go where other people are going. Sit the way other people are sitting. Except for that one fellow standing off to the side who watches all attentively. He has a wife with Alzheimer's, but she is at home where a paid sitter is helping her. He is serving as a volunteer with the dementia clients who are still able to gather in a meeting room like this one in the basement of the First United Methodist Church.

I have not acknowledged this to anyone else, but the idea is present and alive inside of me: *I adore basements.*

And hallways that go to places I don't yet know.

And kitchenettes tucked into alcoves that might otherwise have been closets.

And the sight of pianos waiting to be played.

And the smell of coffee brewing.

And relaxed people speaking with animation and affection.

And the sight of blue plastic bowls overflowing with inexpensive store-bought cookies because there isn't time to bake cookies at home when you are tending to a potential crowd of 30-40 big snackers, and dementia patients are heavy-duty snackers.

Reaching for a cookie over and over again is a restless move that can be satisfied over and over again and affordably, too, if you are buying the kind of cookies they sell at the Dollar General store. These thin vanilla cookies look like they could come in a package of a hundred for a dollar.

I would eat them. I have eaten them. I am the former caregiver of an Alzheimer's patient. When the workload of extreme caregiving takes over your life, you get hungry, and you will eat a store-bought cookie and be glad to get it.

But that's not what's going on here at Respite, a ministry of the church on the corner that I will hear soon described by the minister Lawson Bryan as: "A fresh expression of God's church."

It is supported by synagogues and other churches and attended by people of all faiths and those who have never recognized the Shepherd of the lost, the One who goes in search of all of his missing flock, the One who beckons: "Come unto me all ye that labor and are heavy laden and I will give you rest. Take my yoke upon you and learn from me, for I am meek and lowly and you will find rest for your souls."

That rest is what Respite is offering to the afflicted and to the caregivers of the afflicted, and something unexpected and hopeful is happening. The clients of Respite are stabilizing. Their clinical numbers are improving or remaining stronger than they are expected to be. The caregivers who bring them are exhaling and smiling because they are getting some rest, and they are coming to understand that they are not alone. Everyone is less afraid of what the day will hold for them because they no longer feel alone, and that experience in itself is a powerful transformation.

The volunteers learn and experience something that Daphne Johnston calls "addicted," but I don't think that word does justice to what they are truly experiencing. I am a new arrival here—a spectator today—and what I see is that there is a great freedom for everyone that is, well, enlivening, refreshing, surprising. You want to keep drinking it—this fresh living water of accepting the truth of your own neediness and your own brokenness, to be for a while in a place where it is understood that everyone forgets something in varying degrees, everyone makes messes, and everyone can benefit from using a bib when he or she eats lunch.

It is where the humble, the forgetful, and the needy meet and enjoy time with each other. It is where the volunteers are not differentiated from the afflicted, where everyone wears the same kind of name tag and where everyone is free to hold anyone's hand. In that way it is a fresh expression of church, a fellowship of human beings who acknowledge that performance, appearances, good behavior and a selfish need to grab more free cookies than is polite is understandable when you think you are hungry and can't remember that you ate breakfast or that you will soon have lunch.

Lunch is served. It is a tasty, fortifying lunch—a lunch that comes with the price of admission—twenty eight bucks a day, seven dollars an hour. And if you can't afford it, well, help is available. Just tell Daphne J., whose smile beams assuringly when she explains, "We can help you. We're blessed here."

Daphne has a growing family of her own and a great personality and a great smile and a great colleague named Laura Selby, who has a subtle gift for explaining the inexplicable and a kind of good-bye that will haunt you: ("Our hearts are full!")

Daphne J. moves around the room like some kind of gifted athlete, and this is her playing field. Everyone is a playmate. I smile, because she sets up the day's activities "to wear them out. When they leave here they are tired." They sleep better, you see, and dementia patients are notoriously restless wanderers. Wear them out by playing hard, and everyone gets a better night's sleep.

And they are well fed, but with more than the simple meal that included two desserts the day I was there. They are fed with "worth and purpose" explained Daphne J. who looks to me like she lives out her own sense of worth and purpose daily.

I recall what it was like when I was her age and as passionate about my various causes and missions. I am still passionate but with less fear that I won't accomplish what is meant for me to do as the work of my hands, which means that I am not in so much of a hurry anymore.

I have a different philosophy of living than a woman twenty years younger has—a different kind of energy too. And as I sit and take in the features of this Respite program and wonder—this idea rumbling in the background of my focus in that moment—how much of the success here is based upon this woman's likable personality and drive, her positive attitude, having a Preacher-boss Lawson Bryan who backs her up with the prophetic proclamation which I find believable, "This is a fresh expression of God's church." (The idea plays in my memory all the time now.)

Have all of the components of a successful missions outreach come together fortuitously for a one-of-a-kind success, or can it be replicated? I'm not just wondering if this Respite center for anyone from any denomination can be duplicated; I am wondering how these dynamics of humility and unconditional love can be used all over the place to help people everywhere who are frozen by a fear of being revealed as imperfect and needy.

Daphne J. disappears to manage some kind of issue in a different part of the building, and I send my heart and good wishes after her. It's called praying unceasingly.

I send Daphne a text explaining that I need to leave after only three hours. She will read that message and not interpret it as anything but the truth, which is something I like about her. Being polite, being strained, waiting to say good-bye in person is what people in a world that worries about right and wrong live by. When you have experienced weakness and helplessness and understand, truly understand, that reason is not always trustworthy, you can send a text message and say good-bye and it is simply good-bye. *See you later*!

See you soon.

Hope so.

Later she will send me a lavish message of affection. She wrote, "I love u so much."

Sweet, I thought. *Ditto*, I wrote. And I thought that I did love her already, improbably and truly and not motherly either, but as someone who just enjoys and celebrates the vitality of another person who has a mission and is going for it full tilt. Simultaneously, I wanted to weep with joy over what feels to me like a church where I have always wanted to belong: the human race of weak and humble people who live that way, and have able-bodied volunteers standing at the ready to hold a hand or escort you from one end of the room to the other faithfully in the name of Love.

It is the kind of freedom that the Prince of Love came to deliver personally, and Jesus still calls us to this loving freedom all the days of our lives and where, if we say yes, we can experience rest for our souls all the time day in and day out until He comes again.

There have been times in my worn-out, heartbroken past when I was a caregiver of an Alzheimer's patient and the Coming One could not come fast enough; but while I was at Respite, I relaxed and enjoyed the gift this remarkable program is offering to others in the name of the Prince of Peace. I found I could wait with patience and fearlessness, found there was a great meaning in our shared admission of helplessness and brokenness, and my heart which has known the kind of sorrow and grief associated with dementia-care was forever consoled by their daily farewell to one another at Respite. It is where good-bye sounds like Laura Selby's day's end benediction: "My soul is peaceful and my heart is full."

TWENTY

....

THE FRUIT IN ESTHER'S GARDEN

Esther's grey head with pressed curls moves from left to right slowly as she watches Guin, her daughter, mow the overgrown backyard.

This old Southern lawn is an expansive area marked with rambling growths because no one has lived here in this house for a long time. An unlikely rose bush has dwindled to producing one flower, a few thorns. A hidden tea olive bush releases the fragrance of solitude, giving birth to contemplation and potent visions.

A friend of both women, I am welcome to help with the labor of reclaiming this garden space or simply to abide here--to enjoy the company of mother and daughter--Esther and Guin--as they rediscover each other after living in different states for twenty years. Three months ago, this widow courageously left her Texas home of sixty years to come and live in Alabama next door to her daughter.

News of Esther's coming elicited caveats which varied in content but can be distilled into one maxim: "You can work yourself to death for an old person, and nothing you do will ever be enough."

That expectation proved false, that warning a lie.

People who did not know Esther could not envision her as some kind of person other than the kind that aging is supposed to produce. As if all older people are exactly the same. As if all older people are too much trouble.

I am well acquainted with the care that aging and the deterioration of health brings, but there are also unexpected rewards found in a seasoned person's company. There are surprise discoveries not unlike that spindly rose bush, thin and thorny as it is, still producing a tender beauty. I see this kind of rare beauty in Esther, in her faithful acts of kindness to me, in her contributions to the fellowship of my home, my church, my neighborhood. She is a pure-hearted woman who does not take pleasure in deceit or meanness.

Contrary to the warnings that the quality of my life would be reduced by Esther's presence, my life has been enlarged because, upon occasion, I get to see the world through Esther's eyes. She laughs easily, has a generous memory. She tells me stories I would not hear from anyone else. She recalls people long gone now and who live only because she does.

It is unfortunate that no one remembers how when we were children the more playmates we had the merrier the time. Esther has brought me merriment. Upon Esther's arrival, I remembered that I enjoy making new friends. More work, certainly. Added worry, of course. Loving others always means some work and worry. I have friends my age who are more trouble.

Esther reminds me of this--this older woman. She is more than an example to me, however. I do not see her only as someone old whose life is now more part of history than the present. Esther embodies beauty, and her life bears the fruit that only authentic beauty and its truth provide, which is the gift of letting others rest. I find rest in Esther's company.

Each day, though half blind and mostly crippled, Esther takes a stroll around her backyard garden, reports a discovery, most recently a vine which we have concluded is the last stronghold of an ancient vineyard attached to the back fence. The grapevine produces a musky fruit, the meat unfamiliar and sweet. We call it muscadine, but we cannot definitely name it.

We instinctively want to celebrate the surprise of it, and we watch eagerly for more fruit to ripen so that we can come and taste the sweet produce of this old, old vine. The pressure to make something ourselves--to achieve--is set aside as we wait upon the fruit of this vine to continue its mysterious ripening.

Moving in Esther's pace, we enjoy the tempo of patience, residing all together in a state of grace, discovered in this unlikely garden during this fresh and undemanding time.

TWENTY ONE

....

BROKEN LIMBS FALLING DOWN

W e pass each other discreetly on our regular morning walks. She is a current caregiver. I am a former one.

From what I know of the quality of life she has created with great perseverance for her husband, who has Parkinson's disease, she is a far better caregiver than I. It took me a long time to figure out that I had to become the authority person in our household, and my neighbor assumed that responsibility faster and became a more effective caregiver sooner.

There is another difference between us, however, and it is not just the different diseases our patients had. My daddy had Al, and her husband has Parkinson's. I was a daughter, and she is a wife. It takes a child longer to realize that she must take hold of the authoritative, decision-making position for a parent who can still create moments of lucidity and command attention in the midst of a disease that eventually destroys the illusion irrevocably that he has good sense. My

109

daddy would have called his condition *having no walking around sense.*

Increasingly, I think our ability to connect logical dots out loud for others varies in terms of illusion. We must have a common ground of connecting the dots called reality, but I also think that we are, as a group of people, not nearly as competent—consistently and impeccably reasonable-- or free of the symptoms of dissembling that we relegate to dementia, whether it's called of the Alzheimer's variety or not.

But what committed caregivers do all share—whatever their familial or authoritative relationship to a patient—is something my friend said yesterday, "Heartbreak. I wake up to heartbreak every day."

Heartbreak is a daily companion for caregivers who watch their patients lose mobility and communication skills. Their flesh fails in all kinds of ways. Minds wander and don't come home.

Lurking on the periphery of what we observe are our dreams and images of the ideal life we had planned to live out happily ever after, for all of us had our reservoir of images and fairy tales that we trusted as predictors of what would happen next. Disease, entrapment, and chronic heartbreak were not part of the envisioned story.

Heartbreak is a major part of the story of an adult's life, for you need only live long and love someone to acknowledge the presence of the human condition we refer to with a word that does not do justice to the amount of pain and loss that the word *heartbreak* points to in people.

This current caregiver and I stop to discuss heartbreak. We do this in flat tones, eyes connecting fearlessly—no tears brimming. The conversation doesn't last long. When it is time to move on, I tell her that her complexion is beautiful—it is—and that if she needs me I am just around the corner. She has never called me.

She assures me that my presence is meaningful and helpful and I nod, for that response is the polite answer of a veteran caregiver who knows that she has her own share of heartbreak to live with and figure out what to do with after the event reaches a different time in her life. She refers to her husband's inevitable passing as "when it is over," but heartbreak won't stop being over. The features of the heartbreak and loss simply evolve.

She continues in her direction, which is opposite from mine, and I walk on, aware a-fresh of the clear sky, the flowers in my neighbors' yards, the rampant squirrel population, the encroaching heat, the growing awareness of very dry ground which is signaling the approach of a drought because we have not had enough rain. Trees are dying. On every street I see broken limbs hanging from parched trees. These broken limbs are just out of reach and will fall with a wind.

Sometimes a limb has fallen to the ground during the night. When I see it, if it is the day that the clean-up trucks collect yard debris in the neighborhood, I go into my neighbor's yard and drag the fallen limb to the street so it will get picked up and taken away. (I like to imagine that my neighbors do not even know a limb has fallen—were never dismayed or bothered.) *See there?* I say, brushing off the bark from my hands. *Job done.* Done by someone who doesn't mind cleaning up the broken limbs that keep falling down--falling down.

No one has ever come out of the house to stop me. I have wondered at my own impulse to clean up my neighbors' yards when the broken limb has fallen. Time after time I have done it without permission because the limb was broken. It fell, and there it landed. It doesn't matter, it seems to me, whose job it is. It is a job that needs to be done. The sooner it is accomplished the sooner we can all get on with the job of living with heartbreak and clear skies and faint breezes and a heat that is often a harsh heat but still a reminder that for a while we are together in whatever state of health we have while living in a special place--the land of the living, though in the company of broken limbs falling down all over the place.

I have no gardening talent to justify my impulse toward yard work—toward confronting the broken branches in others' yards. I have only the experience of having been and still am from time-to-time a caregiver who has learned to live inside a house where a limb was broken and took a long time to fall, and I was there and took care of the problem. Now, when I see a broken limb lying on the ground in any one's yard I retrieve it and carry it to where it needs to be.

And, as a graduate of the school of caregiving of a dementia patient where I confirmed what I had always suspected-- that cause and effect does not always have a reliable relationship-- it encourages me to know that when I do this, I always, always feel better.

TWENTY TWO

....

WHICH WAY IS HOME?

We are driving along the gulf coast and have taken a wrong turn. We are headed in what I believe to be the opposite direction of our hotel. But I don't say this to Guin, who is driving, because no one including my best friend ever thinks I know the direction to home. I do not worry about this. The view is lovely—lots of sunlit, achingly clear, blue water. Waving sea grass. Brightly colored houses are set up on stilts--no sign of any oil spill contaminating this part of the gulf shore. No hurricane expected.

The air is fresh, and when I breathe it I want gumbo and fried shrimp and the view from the pier where I will have that dinner this very evening, eventually.

I am hungry, but I am not in a hurry to eat. I know how to be hungry, and I know how to wait. In this moment, I know how to be a passenger.

I am not driving. Guin is, and her brow furrows just as it did when she and my niece Katie were traveling with me in Birmingham. I was driving, and we were headed wrongly away from the Galleria, our shopping destination. Within seconds they were united in their dismay over seconds lost being lost and anxious and determined to get back on track headed in the right direction. I was not. In Birmingham I didn't care that we were lost.

Like then, in the car headed in the wrong direction away from our hotel and along the gulf's shore line, I felt the same way—blissfully at ease. I am content with the unfamiliar view.

"It bugs me that you don't worry about being lost," Guin says.

This comment is more about her discomfort in being lost than it is a real criticism of any reaction of mine to our situation.

"I know," I say, and I can feel the faint hint of a smile on my face. We are long-time sister-friends. Her discomfort won't last long.

I know from experience. More than one person has thought that about me—more than one person has said that to me. It irritates others when you are comfortable being lost.

I do not mind bugging people in these small ways. I used to care in predictable and fretful ways about pleasing others, but now I understand deeply in the marrow of my bones that the small ways that we all expect each other to behave and call normal are not as meaningful as we habitually believe them to be. Learned behaviors and predictable reactions are the cues and cushions that make us feel that we are at home with others and in our own skins. We like to feel at home. When we are lost, we mostly don't feel at home. I lived lost inside the world that Alzheimer's creates for a long time—it

114

measured three years on the calendar—and I made friends with the feeling of disorientation.

Once I got past the years of grief and sadness I emerged as a woman who is able to be lost and not anxious about it. I learned how to live this way while taking care of someone who had Alzheimer's. Dementia presents some difficult problems to solve. Logic no longer is the default dynamic called being home. Familiar cues of memory that buffer the pain of the outside world are cast aside by caregivers of dementia patients. At the time, it feels awful. Later, you find that having learned to live without the buffers of reflexes and memories that can ensconce you in the warmth of familiarity and insulate you from the cold of the outside world matters less than you expect. You can be a little chilly in the world—with people and your environment--and not need to complain.

Small inconveniences are only that. You do not have to fear physical discomforts, really.

You are free to enjoy being lost.

I am free to enjoy being lost more than others prefer for me to be.

"Which way is home?" Guin muses more to herself than me—but she is asking.

It is a sign that she is either seriously worried now or so lost herself that she is desperate enough to ask me.

I have known for some time which way the hotel is, but I don't need to save the day; so I waited. I have never wanted less to be any kind of hero.

"It's that way," I declare, pointing backwards.

"Are you sure?"

"Pretty sure," I replied. I saw a billboard that named the hotel and told us the mileage. I saw it while I was enjoying the view.

She takes my word for it and turns around.

The other side of the street has a different view, and the sun is about to set over the water. It's truly lovely. I imagine that if Travis McGee, a fictional detective invented by John D. MacDonald, had been a real live man who owned a real house boat called the Busted Flush it would be anchored in one of those marinas. If it were really there I would have stopped and had a drink with Travis and talked about his philosophy of retirement, which matches mine. (Travis famously said that he took his retirement in small allotments when he could afford to rather than wait until he was too old to enjoy himself.) Or maybe I took his philosophy and made it my own because I grew up reading those detective stories. My father, who developed Alzheimer's disease during his retirement, introduced me when I was a young woman to John D. MacDonald's books and his famous character, Travis McGee. I never go to the water that I don't remember all of them—the writer John D., the character, Travis McGee, and my daddy—miss them all. Though in many ways they are still here because they are with me. No one really thinks that's a very important idea, but I know for a fact that it is.

Guin does not think of Travis or John D. She is driving with great focus. Her shoulders are tense as are her hands that grip the steering wheel.

"Our hotel is that way," I reassure her. "Really."

"You are not very good with directions," she reminds me.

"That's true," I agree easily. "I have other flaws. Shall I name them?" I ask blithely. It is good to take a get-real inventory of one's flaws from time to time.

She shakes her head and sighs heavily. She is close to not liking me in that moment, and I smile, for that, too, will pass. I learned how to live with people not liking me when I lived with Daddy while he was sick. Alzheimer's patients often dislike their caregivers. Daddy adored me before be started not liking me. I smile thinking about that and wonder what I would drink if Travis were docked right there—right there where the sun's dying rays have anointed the water with such a splash of color and light. Beer. I would like a beer in a frosted glass—or not.

"I see it," she says suddenly.

"Home?" I repeat unnecessarily. *Or maybe it would be a martini.* I like the idea of holding a martini, but I don't really want to drink it. I do like olives—big fat olives.

"Yes. The hotel."

"That sign back there said the hotel would be there."

"You saw a sign. Why didn't you tell me?" she asks, exasperated.

There was a fact, and I did not report it. If I had she would have questioned the reliability of my eyesight and whether I had read the words on the sign correctly. I have learned from experience that it is awfully difficult to prove some facts if they go by in a hurry. I keep a lot of facts to myself because I don't like to talk as much as other people like to talk. That's a fact, and it was a fact before Alzheimer's came into my life, and it is a fact now that the disease has run its course and gone.

"I told you our hotel is thataway."

She sighs again. I am a tiresome passenger today—one who is deeply flawed and smiling stupidly.

I have nothing to prove—just a different way of being in a car and a different sense of what is home and how the change in its location means that you see the world, tradition, memory, and the qualities of a good life differently. *Which way is home?* It's the impulse Alzheimer's patients have as they search for some place that feels familiar. Kinfolk become strangers. A house where they have lived seems like a foreign field. And the effect upon the caregiver is similar. Just as my father paced and roamed looking for a place where he could rest and feel at home, as his caregiver I paced and asked all kinds of questions that were born in his quest to find a place where he felt at peace.

The caregiver asks similar questions, but they mostly go back to that one. Values change as relationships shift—as memories fade. Traditions give way. Days pass one after the other, and in a way you become a fictional character to the other person, invented by interpretation, which causes you to wonder if you had been doing that all along. That's a pretty good question right there: Do we invent each other? Invent ourselves? Make up God to fit what we want God to be? The answer is yes, yes and yes—sometimes.

The boundaries between invention and fact are not as well defined as we all pretend with one another.

One of the things I learned while living with Al in the house is that we who still inhabit the world dubbed normal are closer to the condition of dementia than we think—just not as close as those who have been diagnosed.

I am not afraid of those distinctions--not tired yet of thinking about the questions that still roam across the landscape of my mind, in my memory, in the present, vying for my attention the way my memory of Travis McGee does as we parked at our hotel, a temporary home.

Like a perennial detective, the questions go with me, and the answers, like the solutions to mysteries people read for the satisfaction of discovering that four does result from two plus two, the answers to these questions are not predictable but are fairly reliable. At least, like Travis McGee, they are as true as they can be.

TWENTY THREE

....

I'M NOT DEMENTED
I'M A SKIM-READER

It has been happening too often—that forgetfulness that makes me think, "Uh oh. This is more than a senior moment. This could be That. It could be Alzheimer's."

Some of the worst moments I have kept to myself. I have shared the less dramatic ones with family and friends—*can't exactly remember where I parked my car, left my keys, placed the mail, tucked my ten-dollar bill that used to be called mad money but had become emergency gas money— it's gone.*

When did I spend it? I couldn't remember.

I told those stories to a few people who knew how to sigh or click their tongues sympathetically. *Yes, that has happened to me. No biggie.*

Only there were some biggies, and I wasn't telling those too--big stories because I didn't want to convince people I was developing Alzheimer's disease. I just wanted to kind of see where I fit inside the broad range of how people as a group were losing it (memory, control, spelling!). In the South going crazy is kind of expected in certain ways—not feared either. Actually it's kind of celebrated.

I miss that socially acceptable way of growing older really, because as I have aged I have censored the telling of my Southern eccentricities and become more serious about monitoring behaviors that fit under that scarier heading of "symptoms."

I didn't really tell the scary times when I couldn't remember great chunks of key information, like my confusion about the amount of money for an online fundraiser for the local animal shelter which I was vigorously supporting on Facebook in front of many people who also love animals only to misremember the amount of money to be raised.

I was forgetting what people wrote to me in their e-mails, missing the news of distant relatives who had died. *Really? When did she die? I told you when she died in my e-mail. Didn't you get my e-mail? Yes. I think I got it.* But I wasn't sure.

And here is where we slip up on the truth. I have been hastily managing e-mails because I receive many of them, and in my haste, I have not really been carefully reading all the message. Only I didn't really know that. I thought I was reading them.

I am a veteran reader who grew up on Galsworthy, Tolstoy and Austen. I have always been a lover of reading, only with the onslaught of e-mail, texts and the bombardment of information on the front of every page and screen, I have become something I didn't know I could be or was: a skim-reader. I thought I was reading. Only I wasn't really, really reading every word, so I wasn't really, really forgetting key information because I wasn't really reading content. But I was holding myself responsible for knowing that content.

As a result, I have known some miserable moments of self-doubt and confusion and have done a poor job of tamping down the fear that something worse was happening inside of me.

It took me a while to figure out that so far, that isn't the case.

The first clue that I had become a skim-reader and didn't know it was when I asked friends and relatives to tap the Like button for a Facebook page I supported, and people who loved me ignored me. I could see being ignored by people who don't love me, but when your family and friends don't respond to a fairly benign request, your brow furrows.

I didn't forget to ask them. They didn't forget to respond. There was a breakdown in the communication. The answer? They were skim-readers too.

I wasn't the only one. Apparently, I come from a family of skim-readers, and I suspect that we fit inside a nation of them with lots of people like me unaware of how much we are only skim-reading—and later, when held accountable for the details, don't know them and fear the worst.

The good news? It isn't worse. We just have too much to read and have begun to hit the delete button before we have actually read the whole message.

The answer became clear when a friend of mine told me this: "My book hit the floor again last night. I thought I was still reading, but I wasn't. Finally, the bedside light woke me up, and I realized that my eyes were closed. I was imagining that I was reading, but I wasn't. I was sleeping."

I have been doing a version of THAT—not the Alzheimer's THAT!

The same realization hit me about that dollar amount for the animal shelter. I didn't forget the amount or the rules. I never really read them, but I kind of thought I had, only I hadn't. My eyes moved down the page—scrolling, is what they call it—but I wasn't registering specifics.

When I began to realize that I wasn't forgetting so much as never actually reading what I thought I was reading, a great sigh of relief rose up in me. My word! I am not demented! I have become a skim reader.

I imagine that there are other people out there doing the same thing, keeping the same kinds of scared secrets about how much they apparently have forgotten of what has become common knowledge among other people (although there were a number of us who didn't know our aunt's mother died). Dementia is real. But there is an alternative explanation for some of the behaviors known as "loss of memory" and in my case, it turns out that I wasn't so much forgetting as never reading the whole updates or e-mails in the first place.

I have pushed my glasses up my nose, slowed down my attention clock, and pledged to pay more attention to the flying documents that scroll down my screen so when I learn or think I've forgotten something, I really will have.

TWENTY FOUR

....

THE ELLIPSIS

My mental landscape felt like a desert. Suddenly the words and ideas simply vanished into the equivalent of endless sand. There was no accompanying sensation of warmth, no hot breeze, no parched mouth. Just, for a bit of time that I didn't calculate, my mind didn't connect any dots to each other or string some words together. There was an empty landscape—a blank screen really—and I sat in a chair with my cousin Kevin who waited for me to resurface.

I did. And I wasn't afraid. I just took note of the empty landscape of my mind and said to him, "I went blank for a minute."

"That happens to me too," Kevin said, reassuringly. He watched me affectionately from the other side of his eyes— from deep inside himself where people begin to take note that you could be slipping some but are not sure how much.

I have all kinds of excuses for losing it—or losing myself temporarily. I can get away with saying I am a distracted writer. And not long ago I could say I was an absent-minded professor. But now, upon occasion, I simply sit empty of words. When I do become aware that I had just a moment ago something on my mind to say, I see the nouns I think I want to use moving around like a corral full of trapped horses, and I pray this prayer: "Lord, please set my nouns free to roam the range again."

I mean the range of common discourse--just making conversation.

Strangely I am not afraid of these lapses when my nouns are trapped and the interior landscape is a desert place where time is experienced differently too.

The daughter, granddaughter, and niece of family members who have died of Alzheimer's, I know a great deal about the heartbreak and hard work of someone ultimately caring for me if I become a dementia patient, but I am quite simply not afraid of these moments of wordlessness, of living disconnected from my words: the currency of my business. I am a writer.

Rather, like a detective, I return to my senses and search for an image or a metaphor that explains what it feels like to be unable to stamp with your words the meaning of a moment you are living and which is called your life.

Presently I am thinking of these empty spaces where words retreat as a kind of ellipsis, a punctuation mark that is mainly used to show that some words that could be used are not being used. That kind of explains it, but in the very choice of that I recall working with an editor who patiently explained that an ellipsis had four dots, not three, which is the number of dots for an ellipsis I liked to use.

"Why would it matter how many dots exactly?" I asked.

Blessed

Some words are missing. An ellipsis signified by either 3 or 4 dots explains that, but curiously, they are often the same words, the same nouns. Yesterday I couldn't recall the name of a woman in my Sunday School class, and her name is one I have frequently had to pull up with a bucket thrown into the well of my memory, an image Maxwell Perkins used to describe when he was searching for memories too—he, that editor who shepherded the careers of Hemingway, Fitzgerald and who is that other guy?

I have read Perkins' biography twice, written by a man whose name I struggle to recall as well. His book is on my shelf on the right-hand side, three books down from the top. I love A. Scott Berg's work, the story of Perkins' influence and all of the authors he helped but drawing their names out of my memory well is harder work than it has ever been before. I don't understand why.

Why nouns and not verbs? Why the same people's names?

Sitting at a Christmas social last night, I wanted to mention something about Perkins but couldn't think of his name, and I am tired of making my friends play "read my mind." It is much easier for me just to sit quietly the way people who are hard of hearing often do because they can't follow a conversation. For me, from time to time, I can't enter the conversation because I lose my words or connectors. My train of thought simply goes to a desert place and then comes back.

I muse about it fearlessly, wondering if it is the old thoughts that are just worn out like the rubber on a bike tire gets worn thin and can't hold traction anymore. And I pray for new thoughts that will find a more secure place in my memory. If they do, how long will they last or by their newness will they create a stronger association that will make them more easily retrievable? I think that might be true.

Is it an over-reliance upon wornout thoughts and information that causes the associations to weaken and disintegrate like the fibers on a sponge that have been rubbed too long with cleanser in a sink and finally crumble in your hands? Are thoughts and words like that?

I only know I am not afraid, and I reasonably should be. I know that symptoms like this can lead to something like an Alzheimer's diagnoses or a form of reliance upon others that feels dangerously vulnerable and makes a quality of life miserable. But the quality of my life isn't determined by that. Instead I think the quality of my life is determined by how well I can take note of what is going on, and I do take note of what is going on. I simply have a hard time translating it for others from time to time.

Am I just getting older? Is that only what this is?

And as I lose one form of memory storage will another develop to take its place in the ever-evolving experience of being alive? Sometimes I think that is possible because in my deepest wordlessness I am transfixed by beauty, absorbed by a ray of sunlight on water or the eyes of my cousin Kevin's face, so young and pure still. Transfixed by beauty, I am often so deeply joyful inside all of what it means to be alive that I have no words to explain what people refer to bluntly and without nuance as ecstasy. Joy is sort of closer to the truth, but like other Bible words that don't mean in the scriptures what we think they mean in common life, this joy is a vastness of view like a desert where I feel beckoned and welcomed and fearless and patient--so very patient.

Blessed

This morning I was thinking about the blessed emptiness of patience and the kind of joy that abides inside it. I wondered how many people live inside this space and in this landscape from time to time and have no one to tell them, "I've been there and go there still from time to time." It doesn't feel like a symptom associated with doom. It feels very much and often most like that unction, 'Be still, and know that I am God.' Yes, of all the Bible words and ideas, this ellipsis desert event feels most like that.

Increasingly when I stop pre-word and find myself in that stillness where thoughts and words have retreated, I breathe in the invitation of that sentence. It adds a calm that becomes the joy that I report, but I have only the barest kind of smile on my face to back this up. I suspect that smile looks very much to others like a glazed look of confusion. But I am not confused. I am alive. I am wordless, patient, and unafraid. In ways that the Bible explains I am set free from all of the words that at their best simply can't tell the whole truth about being alive, and I am surprisingly not only joyful but optimistically at ease.

....

TWENTY FIVE

CAREGIVERS EVERYWHERE
I GO

As local bureaucracies move forward to make their states dementia-friendly, I sit in a restaurant that had its origins as a truck stop. Way back when my uncle Tommy hosted his wedding party here at Jim's Restaurant, just four people attended: my parents and my Uncle Tommy and his bride. Since then I make an annual visit (sometimes more) and sit by myself at a corner table and smile benignly at people who smile benignly back. It is a humble dining establishment. I've seen many of its sister truck stops and restaurants along all kinds of roads I've traveled going here and there giving speeches. People like me work here. People like me eat here.

I am at home here with lingerers and loiterers—people not in a hurry to go somewhere else. They are people like old Mr. Ashley from long ago on Alabama Street, who got to feeling better just by going out in the world and having a cup of coffee and a piece of pie at a diner downtown. I feel better after going to Jim's, and then I go over to visit my Aunt Judy or to my cousin Kevin's house not far from here on the other side of a round plot of land that creates a cul de sac where a bunch of goats graze, keeping the grass mowed. There are loose chickens sometimes, and they run over into the yard of the fortune teller who lives on the corner. Not many people go there in the daytime.

"People visit the fortune teller closer to midnight," Kevin reveals. He keeps an eye out his front door where he has taken to waiting for me in his wheel chair, his good right leg keeping him balanced there until I arrive, compensating for the loss of his lower left leg—an event that happened last July. It hasn't changed our relationship. Cousin Kevin still takes care of me when I go to visit. He listens. He laughs. He understands. He administers his one-size-fits-all cure for ailments: sweet ice tea. But when I can't come out of my silence or when I need to go into it, I hang out at Jim's and other places like Jim's.

I pray there, too. My prayers are no longer the girlish utterances of a child who had read Ezekiel before she came of age (whatever that means), and it's been a long time since I heard the angels singing on the other side of a stained-glass window. That doesn't mean my spiritual life or prayer life is diminished. It's just different now. Now, I sit in public places and ruminate about people I have loved, and I love all the people around me, offering them the same nods and instinctive smiles they offer me as they tend to each other.

People tend to each other in places like Jim's. Napkins are tucked under someone else's chin like a bib at the Respite ministry over at the Methodist church. People who are hard of hearing meet people who speak up and ask lots of questions, trying to piece together what would satisfy their appetites like they do at assisted living places and the homes of caring relatives. When someone stands temporarily lost just inside the front door of Jim's, heads perk up all over the place. Before long someone who has the spirit of tender mercy abiding in him or her will point to the restroom or discreetly signal a server dressed in wash-and-go scrubs bought at the local drug store and worn as a server uniform to go and shepherd that would-be diner into a booth. Half the people here will keep an eye on the lonesome newcomer, and someone might even pick up the check. People with thinner wallets or living on a limited income are very generous with what they have. Very generous.

That generosity of spirit is what preachers cultivate with their sermons, but it is what the Holy Spirit sent by Jesus brings to life as He blows where He will, and it would be imprudent and audacious of me to name those places. Imprudently, audaciously I believe He has blown a central truth over to the Respite ministry and that Lawson Bryan named it when he called that ministry, "A fresh expression of God's church." Daphne Johnston and Laura Selby embody that refreshing expression. So do all the volunteers. The back story of Lawson Bryan's Jesus-breathed truth is that we are all meant to be taking care of each other. Jesus told us to do that a good while back when He told a story about a Good Samaritan, a good neighbor and a practical-minded caregiver. Jesus is still telling us in His way from the cross where we go to find out how significant we are to Him, and how He loves us and how He lets us go, too. His is a very interesting love—irresistible, ultimately. There is great hope in knowing that.

This is what I think about at Jim's and at my southern church from time to time and at various assisted living homes and ministries like Respite now and then when I see a lonely piano banked against the wall and want to play it, for when Mr. Ashley died, he left my family a thousand dollars "to buy the girls a piano." I guess he foresaw a time when the angels would sing too softly for us to hear them, or we would move and somehow lose the place where I had listened to the angels singing with him. He was right. Alabama Street was decimated years ago. It exists only in my memory like Mr. Ashley whose gift of a piano created in me a love affair with pianos that I have mainly kept to myself.

You need a little something of your own to hang on to as you grow older wherever you go or live or eat, and I was thinking that and beginning to hum a favorite Nat King Cole tune when suddenly I heard a voice from far away reach my consciousness. I looked up at the server wearing medical scrubs. She waited for me to focus on her; and when she saw that my attention had returned to the present moment, she asked me in a voice loud enough for someone hard of hearing to understand, "Honey, do you need a piece of pie?"

WHAT I NEVER TOLD THE PREACHER

....

BONUS EXCERPT
THE MISSION OF
MILDRED BUDGE

I t's a long way from the pulpit to the pew, and
sometimes there's a chasm of silence that exists
between the preacher and a church lady. Oh, we talk
to him. We shake the preacher's hand on Sunday mornings.
We pray for him. We brag about him to others who don't go
to our church. But we don't tell the preacher everything. We
tell God everything, but we don't tell the preacher.

I think that's fine. I'm not a big believer in sharing your
private life with people who don't need to hear it, and the
preacher has never really needed to hear my private story.
But it exists, as do the stories of church ladies who move

about almost invisibly, the way the aged do later in life--slowly and often unseen and unheard.

Sometimes that unheard status is a kind of holy silence where private lives grow honestly and authentically before the Lord. Sometimes that silence represents a reserve. A sanctified surrendering of will can be mistakenly judged as apathy, but sometimes it is just a form of self-defense, too. It is risky and frightening to be known too well in all your non-glory moments. But when the desire of your heart every day of your life is to love and honor God above all others first and to love others well, sometimes you need to break that silence—risk being known by telling some stories.

What follows are some stories about church life and specifically the work of missions—the Grand Commission (a.k.a. as the Great Commission, but I like Grand better). These tales represent some of the back stories of church life that happen to church ladies, and they represent some of what I never told the preacher.

It's not all of it—just enough trouble and truth for today.

Daphne Simpkins

Montgomery, AL 2018

ONE

....

--PULLING A MARTIN LUTHER

"I was reading Martin Luther's memoir," Mildred said.

"Why?" Fran asked, naturally.

"I don't remember how I came to be reading it," Mildred confessed, brow furrowing.

"Are you sure that's what you were reading? Did Luther write his memoir?" Fran interrupted. Her hair had been freshly done, styled in the tradition of Doris Day but was an enhanced grey, not blond, like Doris'.

"I think it was some kind of sermon, but what I was reading felt like Luther's memoir," Mildred replied. She pushed her brown plastic glasses up on her nose.

Fran stared up at the ceiling, scratching her chin the way her first husband had but her second husband-to-be didn't. Speaking ruminatively, Fran asked, "Do you think sermons are preachers' memoirs?"

"Yes. Many of them are," Mildred replied easily. "Sometimes a sermon is a memoir of a preacher's spiritual growth."

"Don't ever tell a preacher that," Fran warned, unnecessarily. Her blue eyes blazed with conviction. Silence was a church lady's strong suit, especially in the South. Seasoned church ladies did not give up the power of keeping their own counsel inside a deep and holy silence without calculating the risk or the cost.

"Oh, I wouldn't. Certainly not!" Mildred replied emphatically. It was an unnecessary proclamation. Neither church lady ever told any preacher very much.

Fran nodded, comforted, for it is in the small ways that people agree with one another which creates that bond called friendship. Fran and Mildred had been agreeing with one another for years.

"So, you were reading Martin Luther?" Fran prompted, steering Mildred back to her original point. "And....?"

"Bless his heart. Martin Luther said, 'I didn't have much to do with the Reformation. I was having a beer while the Word did the work.'"

Fran grinned at this unexpected report about the Father of the Reformation, an event in world and church history that had just celebrated its 500th anniversary.

"Did Luther really say that? The part about drinking a beer while the Word did the work?"

"Oh, yes, Martin Luther drank beer. His wife Katharina made it," Mildred said. "It was very good beer, or at least his friends thought so. Those two always had a lot of company after they got married. I don't know how she learned the beer recipe. Katharina was a former nun, and I just can't imagine a lot of nuns drinking beer."

"I can," Fran replied instantly. She was a teetotaler, but she understood why others needed or wanted a drink. "Why hasn't some preacher mentioned that little tidbit about the beer in his sermon-ish memoirs from the pulpit? There are a lot of people who would be as interested in Martin Luther having a cold beer as they are those 95 theses suggesting reforms within the church that old monk so famously posted on the church door."

"I don't think Luther's beer was very cold. They didn't have refrigeration back then," Mildred replied, practically. She fiddled with a Band-Aid applied to her right forefinger to protect a series of unfortunate paper cuts that she had acquired after a feverish morning's quest spent paging through cookbooks looking for a wedding cake recipe she could almost remember. Mildred didn't recall which cookbook it was in or the name of the wedding cake, but she thought if she could read the ingredients or see a picture of it, she would recognize it.

"Imagine what it must have felt like to write out 95 reasons to reform the way you worship God in a formal church. Have you ever wanted to write out some messages—the stuff you never say from the pew while the preacher is talking-- and slip over in the dead of night and post your comments on the church door like Luther did?" Fran asked.

Mildred did not answer immediately.

It had been a little over a year since Mildred Budge had stopped grading students' papers and a funny thing had happened to her. She didn't want to grade anyone's papers ever again and that meant she didn't really want to write any kind of reformation suggestion on the church house door. Mildred Budge was content. But she was a friend of Fran's so she maintained a friendly interest in the question. "Other than an occasional suggestion about how to raise money for missions I don't want to pull a Martin Luther at church," Mildred replied honestly. "What would you write, Fran?"

Fran answered immediately. "Put up a handicapped ramp at the front door of the church building so that people with mobility issues can enter the sanctuary the way they could when they were younger and more able. Don't tell me again that we've already got a ramp at the back of the building that is adequate. It's too far to walk. I don't care about the aesthetics of the front of the building being protected either. What I do care about is that moment when you cross the front door threshold into the sanctuary and experience the peace of God. Vespers at twilight!" Fran breathed in wonder. "There's nothing else on earth like the twilight service on a Sunday evening after a good nap. Week after week it's like falling in love over and over again.

"You can't get that feeling just anywhere. You cross that threshold into the sanctuary, and all of a sudden you feel whole. That's when you understand--or remember --what the gospel brings to your life. I want everyone to have that— to have that crossing the threshold experience of remembering wholeness when they enter the sanctuary.

"If kinfolk and caregivers are pushing people in wheelchairs up the long back hallway trying to breathe while hoping their legs won't give out, they don't get that threshold experience," Fran declared flatly. "I want everybody to have that experience of God's welcome. I'd write that down and post it on the church door in a heartbeat—day or night."

Mildred eyed her feisty friend. This was the first time in their years' long friendship that Fran had revealed what it was like for her to enter the sanctuary of the church. Mildred marveled at the confession for it was different from how Mildred crossed the threshold into the sanctuary on Sunday evening. Mildred thought of the times she had crossed over—gone through--and how she had always been aware of the shift from the outside light to that first experience of shadows in the foyer and then looking up and toward the pulpit and the bright lights inside and the lit-up shining faces of her friends—so many friends! But first there were the deacons holding the doors open for her and handing out the Order of Worship bulletin, and sometimes one of the deacons patted her on the shoulder. Mildred always liked those pats on the shoulder. A hello-pat on the shoulder from a welcoming deacon was very warming indeed.

"What else would you write?" Mildred asked, intrigued by her friend's convictions about the unending delights of the gospel.

Fran answered thoughtfully. "I don't want to write down anything else—just that one thing about access to the wonders of evening vespers because it's real important. If they could hear me about that, then I think it would lead them to discover for themselves the other issues that possibly need to be resolved and maybe not. I've lived long enough to know I've been wrong more often than I've been right and that wisdom is sometimes just doing and saying nothing. Sometimes preachers call our silence apathy, but that's not what it is. When you're silent it's mostly because you have lived long enough to know you could be wrong. What would you really write, Millie?" Fran coaxed.

Even between the two old friends there was a reserve, a holding back from time to time.

'God be merciful to me a sinner,' Mildred thought. It was often her first thought about most questions regarding complaint or reform.

Then, Mildred considered writing an invitation to anyone going by the church: 'Come, everyone who thirsts, come to the waters......' But a lot of people who had never crossed the threshold didn't know they were thirsty. She dismissed the idea.

Instead, Mildred said, "If I actually got around to writing anything, I think I would like to write the preacher a thank-you note. He works awfully hard. I see him working so very hard."

"I see him working hard too. And the elders and the deacons. I don't think they'd appreciate us thumb-tacking thank-you notes to the front door."

"I don't send thank-you notes to the men in the church anyway—just other church ladies. If I want a man to know something, I usually just tell his wife. Wives know how to pass along a message more effectively than posting it on a front door."

"Do you think that men at church ever try to pass along ideas to women in the church through someone else?" Fran asked. "We widows and single women would have a hard time hearing a message from anyone, because we don't have anyone through whom the idea could be passed."

"If they tried to send me a message, I didn't get it," Mildred stated plainly.

"Me neither. Never gotten a message from a man at church in my life either. Just the preaching, which is quite a lot."

"Do you ever wonder what a church man today would write on a piece of paper and nail on the front door of the church in the dead of night? Is there anything a church man wants to say to the church leaders that he doesn't feel able to say out loud in a general meeting?"

Fran thought about the question and shook her head. "I don't know, and for all of the times when you and I have discussed the boundaries of speech and service at church according to gender, the Bible, and traditions that question and my answer that I don't know any more about what church men are really thinking than they know what church ladies are thinking says more about me than I expected to suddenly learn about myself at my age."

TWO

--THE GOLDEN RULE
OF MISSIONS

"I have a new idea for raising money for missions,"
Mildred announced with excitement.   She was
standing in the kitchen, the sunlight so bright upon her
shining in from the window that Fran couldn't see her best
friend's face.

"It will work like a dream!" Mildred promised.

"Déjà vu," Fran whispered to Jesus before fixing her face
into the kind of pleasant '*Let me hear your idea*' expression
that Mildred Budge counted on when she started another
conversation about missions at church.   Mildred's best
friend Fran had many expressions that showed up on her face
and which were now etched in furrows and crevices that she
did not try to disguise with powder or creams.   In that
moment, Fran Applewhite adopted the signature expression
her grandpappy had worn when he taught Sunday School:
pensive and kind. "You have a lot of new ideas about raising

money for missions, but they are not always practical," Fran said firmly but kindly.

"This one is," Mildred boasted. "It is one of those golden moments when time and mission meet the here and now."

Fran shook her head. Well-sprayed grey curls stayed firm, attesting to a kind of resilience and persistence often assigned to soldiers standing post. In a way, she was. "What have you been drinking?"

"Just a Coke. Not a whole one. You know I am not supposed to drink Coke."

Mildred had diagnosed Coke as a digestive issue many years ago. She now thought of herself as fasting from Coke, but she drank it rather often. When she did, the caffeine with sugar could cause Mildred Budge to reach a fever pitch of excitement. Fran nodded tolerantly and sat back in her chair and asked, "You want to raise money for missions how—this time?"

"Well, we live in the South, and everyone here still talks about the Civil War...."

"It was the War of Northern Aggression. Surely you have lived in the Cradle of the Confederacy long enough to remember the distinction true Southerners make about our history. Ask Anne Henry. She'll explain it to you."

Anne Henry was the local expert on the Great Waarh and a formidable tennis player. She had the best smile at church but was most famous for not complaining--ever. If you asked her how she was, Anne Henry always said, with zest, "Fine! Fine!"

"I know they have different names for the Waarh," Mildred continued blithely, innocently, too old really to be as naïve as she was about most everything Southern. "But what I mean is that people still like that movie *Gone With the Wind*, and this is where I am going with my idea."

"You have been watching *Gone With the Wind*? Who has time to watch a movie that long anymore?" Fran asked, peering over Mildred's shoulder out the window where life was happening and where people who did not know that real life was found in the vital living presence of the risen Savior of the world walked around like zombies—unconscious zombies. Fran wondered idly if the current cinematic obsession with zombies was some kind of Jungian expression of the collective unconscious and the unconsciously lost who didn't know they were dead in their darkness and were walking fast and going nowhere real because they couldn't see themselves clearly or where they were going without the Light. Fran said none of this to Mildred, whose face was lit up with wonder and hope. Fran loved that about her friend and returned her attention from her post-Jungian theory about zombies to Mildred Budge, who was such an optimist—at her age!

"No. I didn't watch the whole movie. But it was playing on Turner Classic Movies, and I caught a glimpse of that scene where Melanie and Scarlett are at a dance, and they are helping to raise money for the Cause."

"I don't recall any scene in that movie where Scarlett O'Hara raised money for missions. I believe she had other priorities. Ashley Wilkes? Rhett Butler? Saving Tara?" Fran did not add that she had read somewhere that Clark Gable, who played the dashing rogue Rhett Butler, was a good kisser. *'Who was that actress in that movie who said that kissing Clark Gable for the first time made her feel weak-kneed?'* Fran, who understood the wily ways of the flesh, experienced a momentary mental excursion wherein she imagined kissing Clark Gable until her knees went weak, and then realizing that the fancy led to danger, came to her senses, did what Christians call, repent, and with will, discipline, and focus, returned her attention to the conversation about the God-appointed work of any and every Christian: missions.

Mildred was aware that her friend's attention had momentarily split, waited patiently for her to return, and when she did, said: "No, Scarlett didn't raise money for missions. It was for the Cause, the South!" Mildred clarified. "Frannie, you aren't following me. What are you thinking about?"

"To be perfectly honest I was thinking about what it would be like to kiss Clark Gable," said Fran, who had a fiancé named Winston and who, upon more than one occasion, had kissed Fran enough to cause her to experience weak knees and smudge the lipstick she wore. It was a shade of lipstick ironically called Wine With Everything, and Fran was a 90% teetotaler. There were rare occasions when the abstemious Southern belle would for friendship's sake take a sip of pink champagne at the wedding anniversaries of people who had been married for fifty years or longer. But that was the sum total of Fran's relationship with alcohol.

"I've never thought about that," Mildred replied, wide-eyed. "Kissing Clark Gable." She and Fran had been friends for eons—long enough to say "yes" in public to cashiers at grocery stores and restaurants who asked, "Are you two girls sisters?" and had grown comfortable saying, "Yes, yes, we are," and were not lying. For inside the living love of Jesus they were sisters through and through. Only occasionally one sister wanted to talk about raising money for missions and the other sister wanted to talk about kissing Clark Gable.

148

"I can live without Clark Gable's moustache," Mildred replied frankly. "Did you know Clark Gable tried out for the part of Tarzan in the early movies and lost out to Johnny Weissmuller?"

"Why would you tell me something like that? You know how I feel about Clark Gable."

"If Clark Gable had become Tarzan he would have swung through trees wearing only a loin cloth, but he didn't look good enough. That's what they said. When he was up for the part, they asked him to take off his shirt, and when he did he lost the part just like that," Mildred said, snapping her fingers, as if she had been there and seen it happen. But she had only read about it

"You had to say that out loud to me?"

"True is true," Mildred said.

Fran shrugged, her hands going up in a move that was meant to be an emulation of a French woman's world weary shrug about kisses and love and 'I give up being wise; just go ahead and pour me another glass of pink champagne, why don't you?'

"You were saying about missions?" Fran prompted. She returned her attention to her friend for they had been sisters long enough to pay one another the persevering courtesy of considering the other's preoccupations whether they shared apprehension about moustaches or not.

It was Mildred's turn to try and emulate a world weary shrug, but she was too excited to be able to do it with the same aplomb that Fran mustered. "Do you recall in the movie when the South needed money to support the troops and someone goes around collecting the women's jewelry and Melanie and Scarlett throw in their wedding rings to help fund the South's war efforts against that Northern Aggression?"

Fran nodded almost imperceptibly. She wasn't sure, but she was willing to go along with the stated memory. It was easier than watching *Gone With the Wind* again. "What happened at the dance? Was that where Scarlett couldn't keep her feet still?"

"Yes."

"There's a lot of that nervous energy going around," Fran observed dryly.

Mildred brushed aside the comment. "Why can't we have a gold jewelry collection here? A lot of women have gold jewelry they don't like or want to wear, and there's a terrific market for gold these days. We could raise a lot of money for missions in one day of collecting gold jewelry women aren't even wearing and turn it into cash."

Fran was all attention, her head shaking before she answered flatly, "The missionsman won't go for it. The moneyman won't like it either, and I haven't even gotten to preacherman, but he really won't go for it."

"How do you know that?" Mildred asked, not surprised that Fran was attempting to put the quietus on her suggestion. Fran often scotched Mildred's best ideas.

"The concept is too hard to explain. It's got more than three points to make, and you know preachers are trained in seminary to stick with three points about everything they want to discuss. You have to ask for money fast—preferably in one sentence. It's like the Golden Rule of Missions. The idea has got to hit people right in the old bread basket—the gut!" Fran explained, patting her midriff. She was a petite woman, barely weighing a hundred and ten pounds, but given the opportunity she could eat like a hungry sailor. "If the explanation requires more than one sentence and can't be explained in three easy-to-digest points, it's bound not to work. That's one of the reasons that the Faith Promise campaign is losing ground. It takes too many sentences to explain. If it isn't broke, don't fix it, Mildred," Fran cautioned.

"Huh?" Mildred asked. Clichés offered to her as wisdom never seemed to fit the situation she was in, and her very best friend—her very best sister-friend—often didn't agree with her about her biggest and best ideas for raising money for missions.

"Cold hard cash, honey. Our missionsman needs dough to fund outreach efforts in the name of Jesus--not jewelry that he has to fool with."

"We could fool with it. I could take it to one of those places that buys gold and bring the greenbacks to him."

"Now, see. Right there you have another goofball idea. They aren't going to let you go off with a few pieces of jewelry—and it won't be many-- and come back solo with the moolah."

"You'd be with me, wouldn't you? I wouldn't be traveling solo...." Mildred stammered briefly, trying to enter into Fran's rhythm. "With the moolah."

"You don't really know what good stuff is. To you, good-stuff jewelry is anything you bought at its regular retail price. That's not the good stuff. That's costume jewelry just priced high. The good stuff would be worth a lot of money because it's real gold, and the people who might consider giving it would want the good stuff appraised. Then, they would want a receipt so that they could claim a tax deduction."

"Why can't people just toss in some jewelry they don't wear anymore and let the rest of that worry go?"

"Documentation. I don't think the IRS will accept the hearsay evidence of "I threw some jewelry into the plate at church for missions just like Melanie and Scarlett did in the movie *Gone With the Wind* for the Cause.""

"You are making too big a deal out of what could or might not happen. It's a simple idea and a good one—like cleaning out a closet except it would be a jewelry box. People have yard sales to raise money for missions. This is kind of like that, only we are cleaning out jewelry boxes. People don't expect to be given receipts from garage sales hosted for missions."

Fran shook her head sadly, trying for a different approach to explain to her friend what Mildred could not seem to grasp. "What's in your jewelry box, Millie?"

"I personally don't have any good jewelry, but other people do," Mildred confessed easily. She rarely thought about jewelry unless she saw it on other people, and then she thought in a kind of passing way, 'That's pretty.' But she never wanted it for herself except from time to time something glittery like a pair of diamond-chip earrings from Costco that she had tried to talk herself into buying until the young man who was managing the display case that day she had asked to see them refused to show the earrings to her. He shook his head, and said with unapologetic conviction, "Oh, no, ma'am. Those earrings aren't for you. They look like something Dolly Parton would wear." And because she was dumbfounded by such a comment and because she had always liked how Dolly Parton looked—so festive, like a party unto herself!-- Mildred Budge had murmured incongruously, "Thank you so much" and walked away from the good stuff in the Costco jewelry counter. But she still thought about those diamond-chip earrings ($119 plus tax) from time to time, especially when Dolly Parton came on the radio.

"And that's your biggest problem right there, Millie. You are asking people to do what you cannot do. The first rule of leadership is that you have to lead or inspire by example. Do you remember how Scarlett tossed in her wedding ring? Her marriage didn't matter to her so it wasn't much of a sacrifice. You have an idea that will cost others a sacrifice, but it won't cost you a thing because you don't have any good jewelry to toss into the collection plate."

"Is that how people think really?" Mildred asked in wonder.

Fran sighed. "You go think about raising money for missions some more, Millie. I have heard about people collecting aluminum cans for the recycling money. You could do that. Lots of people drink beverages out of cans, although I have heard some troubling reports lately about cans not being as safe to eat or drink from as one would hope. I am going to have to read some more about that one day. I seem to have enough to worry about today," she added, fighting the urge to stare out the window. Some more zombies were walking by. All this talk about money for missions in order to send people to help other people abroad when there were so many zombies walking around nearby worried Fran that day and in that moment.

"I don't drink Cokes out of cans," Mildred replied honestly, following Fran's gaze.

"Not the point. Other people do, and other people mostly throw cans away. You could sponsor a recycling project for cans and sell the cans for money for missions."

"Wouldn't the same principle apply? It would cost them their cans but not me because I don't have any. I don't drink Cokes from cans."

Fran appeared to think about it and then said without a qualm, "No. I think people would do that. I really do."

THREE

....

--LUNCH WITH THE BOYS

When it was Streeter's turn to provide lunch for the Fishes & Loaves Committee, he brought a sack full of foot-long Subway sandwiches and a picnic-sized bag of potato chips that committee members could help themselves to by the fistful and deposit on a spread-out thick white paper napkin on the table top in front of them because there weren't any plates in the conference room where they were meeting.

Eating off a napkin was one of the efficient ways that church lady Mildred Budge ate by herself at home when she didn't want to wash dishes.

"Whaddya want to drink, Millie?" Streeter asked, jiggling some coins in his pocket to signal *I'm buying*. There was a vending machine nearby.

There was no offer of 'Unsweet this or that'-- no crystal pitcher of ice water with lemon wedges.

Mildred replied instantly, honestly, "Coke, please!"

"Coming up," Streeter promised as he walked away and down the hallway of the sprawling Baptist church where they were meeting today—his home church. The Fishes & Loaves committee, which served the homeless and hungry in the city, rotated around to the different churches that had an investment in the multi-denominational mission's ministry and a representative on the governing committee. The rule of the working lunch was simple: when it was your turn to host the meeting, you provided vittles and drinks.

Mildred smiled broadly as the other members—all men--arrived and saw the ample sandwich sections laid out on the paper sacks which had been torn apart and placed as a surrogate table cloth in the middle of the conference room's table next to the hefty stack of all-purpose white paper napkins.

"Grab a napkin and a sandwich," Streeter directed, as he returned with drinks for everyone. He placed them on the table with an easy nod: *Help yourself.*

There was not a gold-trimmed platter in sight—not a doily nor a decorative garnish. Lunch with the boys was so different from the ladies' lunches and which ladies planned so carefully.

Mildred had sat in front of Anne Henry last Sunday night while she had discussed with Lucy, her co-hostess, the menu of a future ladies' luncheon. "Do we want a thinly-sliced turkey breast with Sister Schubert yeast rolls or Pepperidge Farm party-style bread slices?"

Mildred Budge knew the size of the Pepperidge Farm party-style bread slices. It took four slices to make one regular size piece of bread. It was awfully difficult to take and stack eight small pieces of bread to make four small sandwiches in front of other ladies and not appear to be gluttonous. The yeast rolls were just as small. It didn't matter how hungry you were. Two rolls was the maximum number of rolls any lady could take to make a tiny finger-food sandwich. That's what ladies often called their entrees at luncheons: finger-foods.

Mildred had tuned out the discussion between Anne Henry and Lucy about bread slices and rolls before the final decisions had been made for the luncheon. Whatever was decided, the portions would be petite, and the dessert would most likely be tiny pick-up bites of sweets that ladies ate carefully without touching their lips to the surface in order not to mar their lipstick. Often, dessert was brownies or lemon squares not dusted in powdered sugar because no woman who had experienced the mess of white Confectioner's sugar getting all over her bosom in public dared to inflict that danger or temptation on a well-behaved, well-dressed sister, particularly a well-endowed one.

Mildred often skipped the unsugared lemon squares at ladies' luncheons. *Why spend your calories on that?* It was better to go home and eat a bowl of ice cream and pray for people who didn't know how to accept the rightful inheritance of the saints, which was, in part, what dessert was supposed to be, she believed.

And the church lady believed more than that.

Mildred Budge believed whole heartedly in the second law of loving other people as yourself by actively housing the homeless and feeding the hungry. She fed herself with the bread and water from the Bible, fascinated and flummoxed at the same time by the inscrutable beauty of God's love found throughout the story of his love affair with mankind. Daily Mildred Budge opened the Bible and asked the Master of the Feast of Life: *"What do you mean by that?*

157

And that? Feed me lots and lots of manna! No bite-sized pieces of bread, please! I want lots—full-sized pieces of bread! Drench me in Living Water!"

And she always prayed for people who didn't relish dessert and for people who trimmed their azalea bushes into perfect squares. They cut off perfectly beautiful flowers to create a square bush. Bushes like that filled Mildred with dismay—the same kind of dismay that she felt for people who didn't understand why dessert mattered. Dessert was always something one should be able to look forward to! So were flowers in the spring on gently snipped bushes!

As if reading her mind, Streeter suddenly extracted a big bag of M & M's, tore it open, laid it within arm's reach, and announced, "Grab some dessert."

"Merciful Jesus," Mildred breathed, a blessing of sorts.

Sandwiches were consumed, chips chewed, drinks drunk, and prayers spoken as decisions were made and money spent to help the less fortunate of God's children. During the meeting, men laughed a lot and ribbed each other in a way that reminded Mildred of how fifth grade boys on the playground batted a ball around among themselves without fear of hurting one another. If someone did get slammed by a veering ball—or at the meeting, a roughly spoken comment—the other guy ignored it or slammed it jokingly right back at him.

At lunch with the boys, no one got his feelings hurt.

By meeting's end, Mildred was thinking she would just provide the same sumptuous manly, practical sandwich meal when it was her turn to host the Fishes & Loaves committee at her home church. There would be no covered basket with tidy crust-less sandwiches, no peach-flavored artificially sweetened ice tea, and no tiny desserts naked of

Confectioner's sugar. Instead there would be this: fist-sized fat sandwiches with lots of meat and veggies, salty chips, a variety of icy cold, sugary drinks, and colorful M & M's lavishly poured onto the multi-purposed paper napkin from which everyone just grabbed some and popped them unselfconsciously—it looked like gluttony, but it was really a healthy appetite!-- into their mouths. Mildred liked the red ones best. She was just about to blot her lips on her well-used paper napkin when it occurred to her that something had happened at this lunch with the boys that didn't happen at ladies lunches, ever: she was full.

THE AUTHOR

....

ABOUT DAPHNE SIMPKINS

Daphne Simpkins lives and writes in Montgomery, Alabama. Her books are available though most on-line outlets, including Amazon. You can connect with her on Facebook, Linkedin.com and Twitter. She speaks when asked and she can and often on the subjects of Nat King Cole and W. C. Handy, both music men born in Alabama.

Her work has been published in the U. S. and Canada. Her other books are:

The Mission of Mildred Budge, a collection of short stories about church life in the South

Christmas in Fountain City, a heartwarming Christmas tale set in the South

What Al Left Behind, a collection of essays about growing old too fast and how it changes your vocabulary

A Cookbook for Katie, a memoir masquerading as a cookbook written for her niece upon the occasion of her marriage to Levi Shrewsbury

Mildred Budge in Embankment, the second novel in the series featuring a retired school teacher and full-time church lady of the South

Mildred Budge in Cloverdale, the first novel in the series that began with short stories

Miss Budge in Love, a collection of short stories capturing the beginning of Mildred's life story in the South just after she has retired as a public school teacher

The Long Good Night, a memoir about caregiving

Nat King Cole: An Unforgettable Life of Music, a biography for children about Nat King Cole

FINAL NOTE

....

ACKNOWLEDGEMENTS

These days my life intersects fairly often with the younger generation of mostly women who are creating and nurturing caregiving partnerships. I enjoy their energy and commitment—applaud their zeal and willingness to host awareness-raising and fund-raising events while serving and educating the community around them on how to be more helpful to others. It is not a small vocation. It requires a committed love, and I have found that in Stephanie Calvert Holmes over at Dementia Friendly Alabama, an outreach of Central Alabama Aging Consortium. Stephanie found her vocation by first being a volunteer at the Respite Ministry over at the Methodist Church with Daphne Johnston and Laura Selby. I met Stephanie there and have been watching her impact the state of Alabama with her Dementia Friendly vision and efforts to achieve it.

Stephanie's efforts support the ongoing and inspiring work of the Respite Ministry, which is highlighted in the story "Respite for Everyone." Since I first met Daphne, the Respite ministry has grown and multiplied. Daphne has helped to set up other centers like the one in Montgomery and in other cities. Daphne Mobley Johnston routinely speaks at various professional meetings where she reports the success of helping people in all stages of decline adjust to the changes in their lives. Daphne rightly asserts that no matter who you are or what your challenges are, you have worth and purpose. Her team helps people discover and thrive by knowing and living that essential truth. Daphne is a marvel, and I love knowing her. You can find out more about the Respite ministry by contacting her through the First United Methodist Church in Montgomery.

Through Daphne, I met Katie Laing Holland who directs another respite outreach ministry at her Methodist church in Dothan. With zest and commitment, Katie's team serves the members of her community in the spirit of the Good Samaritan.

I enjoy watching and applaud their holy enthusiasm as it spreads to new sectors of an ever-broadening community and look forward to what they can envision and create next as an arms wide open expression of their commitment to and compassion for an aging population and their caregivers.

Aside from these younger leaders, the people in my personal life who inspire me to keep praying and breathing include the Barnabas class where the ladies know how to take care of each other. A special thanks to the wise and inspirational Cam Fox and the hospitable and very kind Gail Clements for welcoming me to the class and keeping me on track. You two Barnabas gals inspire me and to love others better.

So do my sisters. I have three sisters, and you will have seen them show up in various stories in this collection. For the record: Mary Ellen is still the family genius, Patty is the wise psychologist with Princess-like qualities, Julie Ann is the baby of the with the most grandchildren in the family and can quilt and sing and beat me at Quiddler. Katie is still and will always be my Beloved. She married her sweetheart Levi Shrewsbury, and a couple of essays in this book showed up in the cookbook I wrote for her five years ago when she married: *A Cookbook for Katie.*

I am also grateful for the abiding and friendly presence of Sue Luckey's mother Joyce Kelley Asbury who will receive a copy of this book just to remind her that any mother of Sue Luckey's is a great friend of mine, I hope.

Guin Nance's mother was a friend of mine—her daddy, too, but it is Esther's story recounted in "The Fruit in Esther's Garden." Guin takes care of a lot of people, and her Sunday School class helps to take care of a lot of people. When a church talks about the benefits of belonging to a small group they are hoping for the kind of love and compassion that the Berean Sunday School class members show to one another all the time. Guin is the best Sunday School teacher I have ever had and the best friend and caregiver I know.

A good friend and member of the Bereans is Anne Henry Tidmore whose hands are always outstretched to others. Like the Good Samaritan, Anne is a wonderful neighbor; and because she is unstintingly kind and generous, she is also naturally a wonderful caregiver of others.

Sue Luckey, Jennie Polk, and Lori Tennimon are my oldest best friends. Shelby Tennimon is Lori's daughter and Gina Koeppl's niece, and the event of that special young lady's birth is captured in the story "Lori." I understand a love for nieces, Gina. Thank you for including me in the celebratory luncheon for Shelby's college graduation and commissioning as a 2nd Lieutenant in the U. S. Army. I was honored to be a part of that lunch and so proud of Shelby whom I held when she was a day old and to whom this book is dedicated. We go back a long ways, girls, and I look forward to our next time together.

Cousin Kevin Scott Morris keeps me hydrated with sweet tea and funny stories, and Aunt Judy always has the door open for anyone who needs a good chat or a dose of her arms wide open welcome. I'll be seeing you soon, Kevin. Get the tea ready, will you?

If you haven't hugged it out with someone lately, I heartily recommend it. A good hug paints a mighty true picture of the human heart and human needs, and the benefits are enormous.

Daphne Simpkins

Connect with me on Facebook, Linkedin.com or
Twitter.

95629002R00097

Made in the USA
Lexington, KY
11 August 2018